W9-ACU-183

Consequences:
Truth and...

CONSEQUENCES: TRUTH AND...

by Daniel Berrigan, s.j.

THE MACMILLAN COMPANY, NEW YORK, NEW YORK

COLLIER-MACMILLAN LTD., LONDON

Library of Congress Catalog Card Number: 67-12794

First Macmillan Paperbacks Edition 1971

The Macmillan Company
866 Third Avenue, New York, New York 10022
Collier-Macmillan Canada Ltd., Toronto, Ontario

Printed in the United States of America

DEDICATION:

Jerry AND *Carol*—To Say I Love You

As WE used to see done in the older books, I thought that I would write you a letter, as a way of dedicating this book to you. The idea has at least a kind of charm; it may even be useful in my attempt to say why these pages belong to you first of all.

This is the only one of my books to come out of a war, out of an experience which continues to be so painful as to be truly a form of actual combat. We know from the Gospel what this may mean. The Lord who comes among us so peaceably knows that the world is no Elysian field, that history continues to plow its victims under, that men reward in their own way the executioners, the generals, the diplomats —even the Christians. But He knows what His own reward is to be. He knows that in order to turn the evil cyclic blade to one side, He will first of all have to endure its furrow in His own flesh. The first revolution begins here; it means submission before powers and dominations, acceptance of that bitterest and most interior of changes which we name "death." Without this, nothing is possible. Once this has occurred, all things are possible; even that unthinkable thing we name resurrection.

Through His death, we believe that men may still rise from the dead. You and I may so rise. We may, even as I write these lines, with the stench of death heavy upon the air, stand firm at the side of the living, sowing in the contaminated air an invisible pollen of joy and courage and gentleness.

When men have risen from the dead, they are like a risen Socrates— or Christ. Their eyes are full of questions: Why are you weeping? Whom do you seek? Have you believed only because you have seen?

Do you love me? Was it not necessary to suffer these things and so enter into glory?

I believe that our task is not so much to answer the questions, which, in any case, recur again and again whether we like it or no. The real task is to translate the questions in such a way that their import is not lost or evaded. Perhaps what the questions mean today is something like this: Is human life worth living? Does man have a future? What price are we willing to pay to grant man his one chance?

I have given your book the title *Consequences*. The reference is, of course, to a child's game. As so often is the case, the game dramatizes a most serious aspect of life: truth or consequences. Is life capable of truth; is life of any consequence? What are the consequences of living truthfully in the world? What price is attached to the life of mind and heart and hands, the stretching urgent impassioned will to be of use, to be available? What price to place one's body in the imponderable scales of man's fate?

There are, of course, as many answers to the questions as there are men capable of formulating the questions. One answer, or better, one clumsy attempt to formulate the questions, lies in this book. It has to do with what we call resurrection, what other men call by a more modest and simple word—"hope."

I am not seriously concerned at the difference of language. Faith has its signs and countersigns, its checks and balances. And while it is supremely important that there be Christians in the world, it is perhaps no less precious that other men, drawing on different resources, walk at our side on the human road. It is of such men I think when I think of you. Our faith is large enough to include them in our love, as their humanity is large enough to include us in their love. A man does not show greatness, Pascal says, merely by standing at one extreme, but rather by touching both at once.

And who is to say where faith or unfaith ends, when both exist in living men who have the courage to look together in the same direction? The direction I name Man. The capital letter speaks of the mystery that enfolds our flesh and the flesh of Christ in a common web of life and death.

This book includes certain reflections of the past two years, culminating in the diary of exile of 1965. What months those were! In these pages I have tried to convey something of their atmosphere, which was one of terror and loneliness and yet of great freedom. That period and its uncertainties were borne by more friends than I could ever count or indeed repay. And I recall something here I have tried to say on so many occasions—my gratitude for those months. Through exile, I was granted unexpected friendships, a new sense of human rights (and

wrongs) in the Church, a sense of the distance yet to be traversed between abstract freedom and its embodiment.

It was then, too, that I witnessed the tactics of international power
as they bore upon developing peoples. So I came to understand the
Viet Nam war in a deeper way.

From that period in my life, I gained new courage, new resources,
new evidence, to support a judgment which I continue to repeat. The
military adventure we are pursuing with such heat and skill and feroc-
ity against a broken people is an abominable crime against humanity.
The war marks our purpose to kill where we have despaired of healing,
to violate and conquer because we are bankrupt of the resources to
assuage and unite. The war is a cry of despair in face of the destiny
which competence, technological skills, and our own revolution have
thrust into our hands; a vocation, to bind up the wounds of humanity,
to place the gifts of creation where indeed they belong—in the hands
of the poor of the world.

It is of the poor we must think at this hour. I think of them as I
walk the streets of New York reflecting on this letter. I am oppressed
beyond words by the "normalcy" of the atmosphere, by our ability to
"carry on," as though the war were no more than an afterthought at
the edge of our consciousness. We wage war, we dispose of the enemy
with insolence and skill, we publish daily body counts of the enemy
dead; and at home we marry and give in marriage, beget children,
trade, recreate, take the sun, work and laugh and dream. Does no one
hear the hinge of fate, closing in our faces?

The poor hear it, at home and elsewhere. For the poor, in Viet Nam,
in Latin America, in Harlem and southern California, this war is an
issue of life and death. Though the rich grow richer, and great fortunes
grow on a war economy, the poor of the world have nowhere to go,
except deeper into the pit.

The poor know this, and they know something more. They know
that as long as such a war as ours continues, the rich too grow poorer
—poorer in human resources, in everything that counts for a human
future. The emperor can deal with his enemies; but that, after all, is
a savage and inferior talent. What he cannot do is order his own life
in the paths of mercy and love; as his skill grows in the waging of
war, he loses the power to wage peace. His mind dulls; he is governed
more and more by caprice and distraction and impulse; he literally
cannot imagine what human needs are, who his neighbor is, what his
stewardship demands of him.

So it follows that millions of dollars are spent on public parks, on
anti-pollution, and on public beautification schemes. But Bellevue
Hospital is a Lazar House; filthy, overcrowded. The police forces of

the big cities are better equipped, more skilled in defending those in possession. But the welfare departments of the same cities grudge every dollar spent on the poor, and ensure that they pay in humiliation and delay for every cent received. Public services deteriorate, the economy is unsteady, taxes increase, the basic needs of decent food, housing, and education lie farther and farther from the grasp of those whose need is greatest. And the public is assured in face of the plain facts, that it is possible to remove poverty from our society, while at the same time we waste our resources on a foreign war.

Thus our domestic news bears an ominous relationship to events occurring a few thousand miles to the east. At home, privation, moral stalemate, social indifference; abroad, death and violence. Punctual as sunrise, the bombers nose into the dawn, heavy with their burdens of indiscriminate death.

And a rhetoric is at hand for every new crime of war; the plebs vote *yes* to the gladiators, the alternatives to violence narrow, the protestors are marked with official scorn.

But in spite of all this for those who stand with the innocent, for men whose version of justice does not include the right to stigmatize and execute the enemy—for us—is this not a precious time as well as a most painful one? At least this can be said: in wartime, during such a war as ours, men are invited to take seriously, perhaps for the first time in their lives, the testament of Christ. We ponder the Gospel; the texts grow conscious in our hands; the words of the Savior leap into life; the blessing promised to the peacemaker signs our brows. We know, as we could not have known ten years ago, who we are, and what is demanded of us. The knives have prodded us into life.

And this is why we even experience a kind of joy as we live through these days. Much that was once impossible to us is now an actual and urgent invitation. We may yet know, as men have not been granted to know before, what it is to be human. We may come to know it, as Christ learned it; in the letting of blood, or in a vicarious gift, in days and nights of anguish, in the death of the innocent, which we share with all the guilty. Guernica, Posnan, Budapest, Dresden, Hiroshima, Sharpeville, Selma; and now, the nameless villages of Viet Nam. For all of these, Christ forgive us!

We have lived through these horrors. We have heard the claims of power and the bestialities they conceal and connive at, East and West. We have protested executions and tortures and bombings and occupations, whether they were wrought in the name of Western or Eastern ideologies. We protested because we knew beyond doubt that no political system, East or West, is granted a mandate to betray and destroy men in the name of the pride of nation and race. East and West, we have witnessed the evil bargains, have heard the terms, have seen the hangman mount his scaffold. We have seen murder done, we have seen murderers justified and rewarded, East and West.

And the game continues. Its name is our present war. When such a war is waged it becomes clear again that men have learned little from the years of Hitler and Stalin, except a skill in methods of disposing, according to methods perfected by other systems, of those who say *no* to war and war preparation.

But if the executioner seems immortal, there are also the victims. And theirs is an immortality of a different order. It is to them we turn, to the noble ecumenists of man; to their prison texts, to their deaths. And beyond.

Beyond to what? Perhaps even to a resurrection.

Such a happening even Pilate could not prevent. Is this not the defeat of the commissar, that he grants immortality to his victims; so that we, even we, may stand with them, and draw on their heroism?

With Delp and Bonhoeffer and Lorca and Leynaud, with their help may we too live as men live who are determined simply to be men.

There is not much more to say. This book, the record of a few years, is no more than a handful of bread cast on dark waters. What counts after all, what stands under God's judgment, is not this or that gesture, but the quality of a continuing life; the work of peacemaking, unity, freedom, responsibility, truth; your lives, which I love.

This gift comes to you like a bird to the figurehead of the ark. On some other day, may it leave your hands in an irresistible surge of bravery, having seen what neither you nor I could see—the deluge receding, the land in sight!

Daniel

Contents

PART ONE

Journey Toward Fidelity

I

Trading in one talent can be a noisy thing, as the single coin rattles about in an empty metallic life. In contrast, the gentle effortless flow, not of currency but of the spiritual energies of life, on the part of those whose existence is the tipping of a great available vessel—"And the house was filled with the odor of the ointment."

Some make of the faith a kind of lofty Olympian tundra where they tread and breathe an air too cold and pure for ordinary mortals. Such heights allow one to dismiss with contemptuous ease the common man's expectation that Christians too will take into account "justice, and the law."

The pure in heart are in the nature of things defenseless. Before the world. And also before the Church.

One lives in a room after a while, with an eye to his grave. The furnishings are unimportant. So, after all, is the view.

"When time has made all equal. . . ." Which, of course, time will never do; it only offers occasions for a more complex structure of injustice. The key: the end of time.

The attitude of faith is no more easily described than a glass of water: colorless, tasteless, odorless; but still, mysteriously refreshing. And when held to the light of day, a prism that captures all the delight and mystery of the world.

Several figures of the Church seem to verify themselves in turn throughout history: the church as House, the church as Exodus. One, the "dwelling" figure (Pauline, perhaps by way of the Greek view of the universe as *amplissima domus*): Men build when the times are kind, when a certain overflow in nature and life offers a pause, a measure of freedom from mere subsistence, a universe that is "benign and ample." Secondly, the Exodus figure: Wars, famine, destitution, personal sinfulness, exile in

3

Babylon, the necessity of leaving the "low-vaulted past," the transcendence and uniqueness of the summons (from what direction coming, in what direction leading?). These are perhaps features of the Exodus image.

A third image seems also to perdure; it is large enough, and mysterious enough, to express the opposition contained in the other two. "You are the Body of Christ." The body—open, permeable, needy, in service, at rest and on the road, beset with suffering, growing and becoming, contemplative and creative, unique and generated. The metaphor implies man's personal body, jealously protected, cherished, fed, and clothed; and it implies man as a world body, acknowledging his debt to Mother Earth with every breath, and always foreshadowing in his poverty and dependence, the day of return, the dust yielding to dust.

As early as Feuerbach: "Individual man does not contain man's being in himself, either as moral being or as thinking being. Man's being is contained only in community, in the unity of man with men, a unity which rests, however, only on the reality of the difference between I and Thou."

"The characteristic of greatness is the carrying out of a will which goes beyond the individual. The great individual knows what the nation's will should really be and carries it out, because the force and capacity of infinitely many is concentrated in him. There appears here a secret coincidence of the egoism of the individual with the greatness of the whole" (Burckhardt, *Reflections on History*). True so far as it goes. And moreover, a profound critique on Nietzsche's unlimited "will to power" as an ingredient of greatness. One reflects— (1) Given the corporate nature of mankind, and its growing consciousness of being corporate in all phases of life, a decision, however enlightened and far-seeing, is of little value so long as it is arbitrary and unrelated to those in the grouping; (2) Burckhardt's idea seems related to the principle, medieval and ecclesial, "What is of import to all, should be discussed and approved by all"; (3) The greatness of decisions and ideas is to be measured by their availability, rather than by any striking originality or thrust of power, by their ability to express the unformulated, obscure hopes of many; to seize upon and vitalize human life, a new soul for an old. The aim of great ideas or great art or great policy, is incarnation, embodiment; a new man, a new form, a new community.

That styles of religious life are changing is news to no one. It is no longer really important to defend change, or to accept change. What is crucial, and will be for several years, is the effort to understand the nature of change, and to act in such a way (both as subject and initiator of change) that what is sacred, real, valuable, comes through as new world and new Church. The task is of course very difficult. One is simultaneously subject to change and yet must bring change about. There are no pure spectators, and yet there must be enlightened observers; in a way, we must be Protestants at a catholic process.

Certain things will always endure, if change is not to become chaos. There is no need to become dogmatic here, or to compose a new chain of "things to be believed." The real point is living faith, charity, a Christ who is present. And from the human point of view, the retention of good humor, courage, suppleness of heart, openness to conversion, inwardness. Literally everything else is worth sacrificing for these. And these cannot be sacrificed for anything else.

What must be prepared for, and actively experimented with, is the creation of new forms of life. And there is no reason why such experiments, such active tribute to the unknown, cannot be paid within the framework of the old. For the old is a nest of the new; and unsuspected life is always longing to be heard, and to be heard from, within the old.

One will always respect the truth of tradition, at risk of becoming a mere destroyer. On the other hand, the Gospel nowhere urges us to remain within a decaying nest.

It is remarkable how new forms of life continue to come to us, like unsuspected hidden springs, from within the most unpromising and suppressed areas of the world; one thinks of Christians under Marxism today, and of what they have had to say to the whole Church. And one is led to think of the ambiguous play-acting that goes on among Christians in the West, the poisoning of the air to which we contribute, the arrogant assumption that "the others" cannot produce art or disinterested research—or indeed a Church. Meantime, the Spirit breathes where He will.

Bonhoeffer speaks of a "sense of quality." The development of this sense has a price tag attached. It means developing a sense of the genuine over the merely phenomenal, of reserve over assertive speech, of listening over persuading, of reading and reflection over sense stimulation, of the individual over the big gain, of suffering and submission along with action, of prayer along with initiative, of anonymity over headlines, of personal change over bureaucracy.

A sense of mystery as contrasted with a devotion toward magic. Mystery is effected, according to Catholic belief, when a symbolic activity, quite modest and concrete, brings about a meeting of two freedoms: the divine and the human, and the opportunity of creative change in human life, a climate of choice. Magic, on the other hand, announces an automatic possession of the divine by humans, and its manipulation toward human ends: the genie in the bottle.

The renewal of the life of faith can be seen from this point of view—it must be purified of its subtle magical appeal. The test of whether mystery or magic is at work will always be the changes being wrought in the community itself—its tightening into a closed fist of selfish exclusivism, or its gradual opening out on the will of God and the hope of man—at whatever cost. Magic costs nothing, except in the tender of a given society; one pays his entrance fee, becomes an initiate, and in every formal activity reinforces his sense of belonging, of earning salvation through bribes, and of excluding the "impure." But mystery creates the individual and his community anew; it breaks up the old molds, forces open hearts and hands, introduces the mind to the real world, awakens responsibility toward it.

Properly speaking, magical rites have no symbolic content, no depth. Their pretension to the miraculous really leaves no distance between the god and the initiates; there is no task, no journey between the divine and the human. So magic ends by destroying those who place their trust in it, because it falsifies human life into a closed circuit for those (literally) lucky enough to be in touch. Magic allows for no growth, no pain, no human response or cost. There is no incarnation in magic, for incarnation implies the ultimate tribute to man: an entrance of God into what is unfinished and therefore perfectible by human hands. Magic leaves us only the indistinguishable dream world of the *Odyssey:* Gods and the humans couple and wage war and connive; a classic cosmic impurity rules everything.

Holding on to mystery, on the other hand, means precisely *letting go.* "Cast off into the deep." It is only a very mature community that is worthy of being trusted with the mysteries. The early Church understood this. An adult community had come to the faith by way of a profound world experience. It was to be thought that within Christianity, the world experience would continue; under a different aspect, of course, but inevitably.

How different our situation today! The conscience of Christianity has permeated the world, the world has even gotten beyond Christians. Many unbelievers surpass Christians in their purity of outlook, their sense of reality, their sense of the neighbor. The protest of *The Deputy,* the Negro revolution, the social gains made by Marxist societies, are extremely unsettling to a society of believers that thought it contained and expressed the conscience of man, once and for all. Being a Christian needs redefining in every age; and every age hesitates between two great choices: that of insecurity in the world, and that of a security that merely draws on what has gone before, and remains on safe ground. The real effort, never really done with, is to discern what Christ is saying to us from within the real world. . . . All else is a mortician's job, or a child's game.

Change is always painful; at least part of the pain is the effort toward agreement on what needs changing. Almost everyone has his own version of what should be swept aside, and of what is worth saving. It takes little insight, however, to see that every form of triumph, even of sacramental or liturgical triumph, is only another bind. Nor to see that the proliferation of Christian projects, structures, groups, is in large part an obsession of security, a thicker wall about the in-group.

We are possibly moving to a point where the effort to verbalize mystery is becoming more and more self-defeating. The world is too much with us; too complex to box, too omnipresent not to threaten even the most tentative statements, especially when these are put in the way of religious claims. To live the faith is the point.

What leads we have from Christian lives that are making no claims are a sort of radiant symbolic activity. That, first of all: no proofs, many signs. World issues are quietly assumed to be religious issues, or, let us say, Christian issues. And one puts his life into that breach. This is also a clue as to why the most viable theology of the last twenty years has come from (1) those among the priest-workers who left a few letters and notes, and died before they were heard from; (2) the prisons of Hitler; (3) the theologians of central Europe. Much of the rest smells of some obsession: to speak in abstractions, to attempt a presumptuous synthesis, unaffected by suffering and exposure.

The world says it needs only itself, needs contact only with its own deepest instincts, in order to run its own version of providence. Empirically it cannot of course be proven or disproven that the world has resources to heal its own wounds and to arrange its own future. And Christianity at its best has not been overly interested in proving anything about itself, or the character of its mission in the world. It has announced a mystery: the divine gift, forgiveness, hope, eternal life.

Each use and teaching about the sacraments that merely announces a divine activity as such, is a perversion of the will of Christ. Each use and teaching about the sacraments, on the other hand, that attempts to embody human hope, to lead the facts and struggles of life beyond themselves, is a service; that is, a liturgy. The first tactic announces an ahistorical God, an idolatry, the Christian obsession to be "out of it," to create a God who is himself "out of it." The second tactic announces the incarnation principle as a continuing fact, the God who is "in it." Thus, baptism must embody conscience and responsibility, and the eucharist must summon men and women to sacrifice.

The critique of Bonhoeffer and his commentators concludes that with the forward movement of history, God has been proven more and more "unnecessary." Man has passed through one stage of growth; God as overseer and guardian is dead. So we are in a better position to see what He was from the beginning. The statement, taken in the sense that His relationship to us has altered, is not offensive to believers.

And what is the basis of a new, mature sonship that is looking to no false hopes or props? that is looking to be only son and brother, in Him? For it seems that faith in God is at its purest precisely when man is closest to asserting his freedom, his whole-ness, his domination over creation. At such a time he has the chance of a real choice of God, one at greatest distance from "thunderbolt religion"—a controlled, mature, fully conscious faith.

One can protest that we have as yet no solid reason for assert-ing that man, in his personal and social aspects, is about to fulfill all the postulates of maturity. The new societies and the "new man" of the Marxists have had no sufficient historical testing as yet to prove they have made it, or that their new societies have made it. And the dominion of man over nature, claimed by science, would surely have to include freedom from suffering, freedom from psychic disorder, from social selfishness, the acknowledgment of a minimal human chance for all men. It is by no means clear that the blueprint is about to be realized. Man has not as yet created himself in any real way, as "new" man. As the first generation of Marxist ideals fades, and as East and West tend to homogenize, we are seeing that the "new" man was largely a historic exception, created by the enthusiasm of a new start. But it is at least doubtful that he can reproduce himself.

In a time when so much is in question, and when the best men seem to question most deeply of all, it is good to recall what was seen as essential by the first Christians; not by way of cowardly regression but of an effort to touch the springs of our being, "our fathers in the faith." When all has been said, the Christian is a man; he knows that Christianity has never scouted or despised the simple requirements by which men live—justice, altruism, conscience. But he knows that these gifts do not make the Christian. He waits on God. No effort of his own can effect the "difference"; no boasting of his can assure it.

For this reason a Christian is unassertive and modest; he knows that he stands under judgment, and that the love that summoned once, gently and irresistibly, may one day be drowned out. "Today if you hear His voice, do not harden your hearts."

The opposite of love is not hatred; it is indifference. When we have learned indifference, when we are really skilled and determined at the business of ignoring others, of putting our own well-being, our own options, first—of thrusting our own ego into life, as the ideal form of life itself—we may be quite certain that at that point, life has become hell. We need be no more thoroughly damned.

Christians without personality. It is as though not the world, but their faith, had choked off everything living in them. Which is, of course, impossible. What has happened, more nearly, is that they have fastened on some form of cultural or sensual substitute, which has gradually sucked dry whatever living capabilities their faith would have brought to flower. What is left is a shell of dreams and phantasy. No heart, no mind, no horizon. No sense of the direction or intensity of life around them, or of the response expected of a man of faith, who knows that faith is destined to incarnate itself or to die.

What form of life will summon men as powerfully as war does? will attract them, unify their energies, make of even the most nondescript among them, for some few hours, a very lion? Religious passion, except for some few, has been no substitute. Neither have ideals of public or intellectual service. All of which is not necessarily a judgment on these latter; under proper stimulus even a nonentity can put on a lion's skin and play his part ferociously. And the instinct for violence lives so nearly under the skin as to leap into action with the slightest provocation.

When all this has been admitted, it remains true that religion issues no more than the most vague and tardy summons to heroism. What it offers in its sermons and the embarrassing evidence of Christian lives, is a way of evasion, a quiet moral minimum, a blameless, passive life by the fireside. Not to be wondered at that few have the clairvoyance to get beyond all this to the fiery summons of Christ.

Apart from the state and the bloodline, there are very few loyalties to which men feel bound to cling today. In normal times, one's bonds to the state are inert and meaningless, a response to minor annoyance—keep traffic laws, pay taxes. Blood loyalties are another matter. Who has not seen even the least passionate or concerned parent transformed into a fury when family values (money, security, the tribal good) were challenged by a son or daughter who had come to see something beyond?

When loyalties of spirit grow weak, loyalties of blood become consuming. To invoke gods other than those of the tribe is assumed to be a sacrilege against nature. And of course a sacrilege against idolatrous nature is exactly the form Christian virtue must take in such a case. "I have come to set husband against wife and brother against brother."

Even the best of our theologians have not shed much light on the nature of revolution in the Church. And least of all when revolution implies the duty of blessing unpopular causes and urging their value on Catholics. We are assured, rather, that the Church will not grow hotheaded or yield her tradition into the hands of the impatient. All of which is a way—more civilized perhaps, but hardly less damaging—of tipping the weight in favor of prudence and reaction. Which hardly allows for a profound analysis of the workings of spirit.

Against a call to single-minded obedience, there is no end of obstacles, even of those that call themselves sacred. They amount to an unscalable, massive roadblock; is it not wonderful that all but the most courageous lose heart? But in the final analysis, the same Christ who calls must create the response; obedience is a gift, not a human capacity.

The Christian failure: not to confront men with choices. But it still may be a providential irony that many of the real choices today, on behalf of God and man, are made outside the Church.

Christianity has always implied responsibility toward structure. From the beginning, the Apostles took others in charge—their human welfare, their worship, their conscience. So there were choices at hand, and adjustments to human weakness, even the presence at times of a pernicious spirit, of mistakes that cost dearly. But our situation is not comforted when we consider the early Church, in spite of superficial likenesses. The average conversion when believers gather today reveals the anomalies. We indulge in the good common small change of an in-group, concentrating on money, good order, and gossip. We are obsessed with the well-being of the inheritance, without seriously considering whether in fact it ought to be spent abroad; most terrifyingly of all, we consider the sacraments and Mass in exactly the same way as a lawyer or medico looks to his accounts, his regular returns, his expanding accounts.

A church with place for sinners?
A church which serves the poor?
A church which is itself poor, as contrasted with the group which gives some hours a week or month to "going down to the poor"?

It is said sometimes that we must match our apostolate to the poor by one to the urban and suburban rich. Give equally good priests to the affluent, and equal results can be predicted. . . . But the theory neglects the facts of life. Who or what in Christianity can help the rich become poor in spirit? A priest who serves the poor with any seriousness cannot fail to become poor in spirit. But who will teach poverty to the priest who serves the rich?

In question here is not poverty and riches at all—but the quality of faith that governs a life. And who is to say in any case that priests generally have more faith to communicate than the faithful do?

Interpreting the call of Jesus, in all its pressing historic complexity: the anguish of choosing among the mysterious good things that the Gospel offers us; the fear of choosing, the fear of not choosing, the fear of inevitably choosing badly—all these are relieved when we choose according to the *sensus ecclesiae,* the Spirit of Jesus, speaking in His body.

But where is one to come on that consensus? So vast a rhythm governs the consciousness of the Church that the wave of knowledge and holiness gathers to a crest only with extreme rarity, once or twice in a century perhaps. And what if the gathering wave does not meet my insistent need? The Spirit who speaks in the whole Church, in the hierarchic Church, in the sacramental Church, speaks in every Christian. In me.

A false literalism demands that we become what we are not: contemporaries of the historical Christ. An illusion. A true literalism demands that we submit to sonship: as contemporaries of living men in the one Body. Reality. Right use of the world implies the willingness and capacity to be used by the world, as God's man.

Does God live on in the believer? Does God live on in the world? The "signs" seem to be correlative; it is not possible to accept one hypothesis without accepting the other.

"To be free of this or that . . ."—always, of course, as a way to freedom. Which is possibly the heart of illusion since in the nature of things freedom is bound up with a certain undissolved slavery.

If one were free to be in every respect the man whom his sins prevent from coming into existence! This is the nub, the reality of guilt one must stay with. Man can only touch or taste his sins remotely, from afar—which is a curse of the state of sin itself. And he touches his sinfulness in the moments when he knows beyond any doubt his refusals and selfishness. This knowledge is, on occasion, quite concrete. Man's sinfulness, at its worst and best, confronts the radiant love of Christ as a disease is touched by health; or, more intellectually, as one absolute opposition touches another. What happens then is part of a continuing unresolved process; I believe in His healing. . . .

The act of faith is colored and made concrete by Christ—both as Act and as Thou. He draws one to faith; faith is in Him. He stands as healer; He acts as healer. Healer of what?

The sensual games one plays:
Self-love, a corollary of the esthetic, insofar as this has not yet confronted Christ.
Despair, hallucination, unpurified ambition.
Fear of the future, fear of the demands made on health by a virile dedication to others.
A demand for freedom, an insisting on its presence, without being willing to pay, or even to discern clearly, its demands.

A moral life based on quality invincibly joins one to Christ and to community. Such a life also implies, inevitably, a sense of mystery whose presence to one's inner life is signaled by signs, hints; one can never, strictly speaking, "rule in" or "rule out" either God or man.

We find it more natural to give ourselves to a performance than to a principle. This is why the God of history reveals himself in act: *Verbum Caro factum . . . crucifixus pro nobis.* . . . Theologizing comes later, and is natural and needful. But in the Gospels,

God reveals Himself by action. Almost in the dramatic sense—
on a stage which widens its arms to include.

"Creating and recreating our spiritual destiny piecemeal, as
we go along" (Henry Aiken, *Reason and Conduct*). Not as
though nothing were given. But as though nothing were given
until it is taken. The horrendous possibility remains; that is,
of leading such an outside, formalized life that even persons
and sacraments are no more than enticements on a tree of life.
And on the other hand, nothing is really possessed until it is
given. An instance of the final, adorable mutuality: "I am in the
Father, the Father is in Me."

One knows others, one loves and experiences others. One can
live in a room, content in the thought of his friends. But one
must also break free into the world, a bodily presence, affecting
and affected by. The world "groaned in travail" for the Incarnation; as the garden was a perpetual autumn, until man.

To share in the tragedy of man: sin, malice, despair, the
plenary horror. To share in the works of God: life made bearable,
the partial resolution of the tragedy, the cry rising from our
hearts to Him, the "unutterable groaning of the Spirit in us."

Clairvoyance: "This will come to pass."
Abnegation: "This will come to pass, but not through me, nor
in my hour."
Faith: "This will come to pass, through God and in His hour."
Resolution in hope: ". . . which I submit to, as my hour also."

Man's sense of sin is often adolescent, abstract, unproductive of
change, of holy fear or renewal—an inverse of his sense of God.
Man is creator and victim of the plateau he lives on; its killing
monotony, its mirages, its emptiness. And when he dies, he has
added nothing; assumed to the landscape, one with it, a zero
within a zero.

A sense of being, altogether compenetrated with a sense of
being inadequate. To be at all is, in the Gospel sense, to be blind,

leper, beggar, to live in a ditch, to throw up one's miserable
dwelling and have the storms bring it down again. But who or
what can help a Christian come to a sense of this, unless God
Himself? A sense of the precarious misery of life, the fate of the
majority of men, joined to the spiritual capacity to realize the
meaning of such life, as ground for salvation.

Sin: the shaping of a heart without capacity for God; in a
sense, incapable of God.

The breathing area of freedom, and the discipline of obedience;
both of them radically necessary in an age such as ours. The best
men are proudly and passionately conscious of their dignity, and
speak a great deal of their need of freedom; but in so speaking,
they express without saying it their longing for obedience, for
someone to give themselves to, for a communion and friendship,
for a counterpoise of thought that will contain, interpret, and
direct their experience.

Authority is an organ of the authority of Christ when it too,
and more deeply and perhaps at greater cost to the one who
obeys, is obedient to Spirit.

Tradition is brought to bear on the present when the imagination of Christ lives on, both in men of authority and in obedient
men. What does it mean to live in the real world? The question
is one that the Gospel both answers and refuses to answer.
Answers in the world experience of Christ, in his obedience and
release into time. *Refuses* in its open ending: "Live on in me,
as I in you. . . ."

Authority which takes on a special style of life, or demands
immunity from the fate of the majority, can never hope to ask
the right questions, let alone to answer them.

A formula for fanatics:

(1) Conceive a principle.
(2) Baptize its Absolute Claim.
(3) Ignore its performance.
(4) Canonize it.

A temptation of great men in face of the inevitability of death: to place some act to which their memory will be indestructibly attached. The absence of this temptation—an absence of greatness? Not necessarily; perhaps death, which is another name for the hand of Life laid on us, has already begun his purifying work.

The history of the world; the transformation of matter in spirit, the increasing availability of spirit. So true is this that forms of performance are either equivocal and destructive (where existing apart from spirit or in conflict with it) or merely useful (as dwellings and structures for spirit).

Why a Christian depends on the intercession of others—not precisely because he knows his own unworthiness (the question has little interest, either before the believer, or before God; an inert fact) but because only the "cloud of witnesses" can express in worthy measure the value of the "strong cry and tears" of our Lord.

The living space in the iron cage—"I am with you all days."
Placing ourselves in the Church, placing ourselves in the world.
Is this not a formula of faith; to realize the depths and height and breadth of this compenetration?
To place one's self in the world, not as passive integer, but as witness; source of new life, of vision, of the service of God in time.
Placing one's self there by submitting to be placed there; a man of providence, neither rebel nor idle servant nor vagrant innovator.
Constantly exploring and enlarging the known frontiers of the Kingdom, the visible geography of spirit, so that the Kingdom is not a limbo of the restless disembodied, but a community of incarnate consciences.
As prophet, from above; as servant, from within. Teacher and taught; man of communion, man as listener.
Agent of faith in the Transcendent, a faith that includes the world.

In how many ways one must consent to live at the edge if he is ever to reach a true center! In order, that is, to become recog-

nizably Christian, accepting the new life as a gift, not as a bribe
or a muscular achievement. And in order also to help the Church
become recognizably Christian—not as an exercise in rebellion
or public rhetoric, but as an epiphany of one's being, a postulate
of love. This "edge" is where Christ is found. It is also the only
true center, the "still point." The only locus of the new creation.
"Come to Me."

One comes to Him, not by moral integrity nor a lighter yoke
of law, but by a submission that tries, destroys, and fires anew
one's being.

What may count as apologia is that in the twentieth century
a certain number of Christians did not give up, in spite of all
provocation to do so. On the contrary, artists became artists;
writers, writers; scientists, scientists. And in their troublesome,
exacting, and dedicated tasks, they were supported by the Church,
which did not condemn or put heavy or untimely burdens on
their consciences, but trusted them as sons. And in this enterprise,
the honor of Christ and the needs of men were served.

But reading the story of Teilhard, how much of this ideal was
violated! And how much honor and service undone, because
many good men who lacked his fiber and faith, simply disap-
peared so far as unusual gifts were concerned.

How necessary the healing work of the Spirit is, in those who
are called to obey; and much more so, in those who command
intemperately.

Who can unite the terrifying divisions of human life, except
only Christ? or the terrifying divisions within the person? One
who has not sensed these divisions to the quick, and sensed their
parallel character, can have little idea of the horizons of Christianity. We are going so far as to say that work done on behalf
of unity, even by those who are unconscious of Christ, or who
are against Him, is still done in His Spirit. He draws together the
world's limitless volcanic energies, its power of creation and self-
destruction, its marvelous intellectual gifts, its biology and spirit,
its suffering, violated, and hopeful flesh. And His action, it goes

without saying, has nothing to do with the procedures so loved by this world—by the officious, the bureaucrats, the specialists of overcontrol, the trainers of rebellious beasts. But in a mystery, within and without simultaneously, as spirit always acts on spirit: within, a gentle unkillable Immanence that is patient, unfearful, viable; that approves life in all its unpredictability and beauty; without, the invitation into the end of things: Come. A victory to assure our victory. A transcendence to vindicate his immanence. A person to modify and breathe on human systems. One impassioned of community, as a man is of his body, as a bridegroom is of the bride.

The appeals to "what Christ would do if He returned," strike one as rather crude and beside the point. The village rabbi could not of course return any more than time can be rolled back on itself. And the Risen One has never departed; only His life is now, and until the end, a mutation in existence. So our appeal to Him as sign is always modified by His presence as reality: Sacrament, community, the substance of history itself attests to Him. . . .

All of which does not make the task of fidelity any the easier; it only places it under a mystery. Does He communicate with the believer? Yes: "I am with you all days." He has become a life-giving spirit. "Whenever two or three are gathered together in My Name, I am among them." Fidelity to the mystery means fidelity to the One who is present neither as memory nor image nor law, but as Event in all events, Man in all men, victory beyond all defeat, a continuing defeat and a delayed victory.

Willingly to pay the cost of living in the real world—a world that is comprehended, even exhausted, in Christ. But to grow into Him, as the price of knowing Him at all, rather than identifying with this or that cultural or religious counterfeit.

"I am ready for today, if you are ready for the day after tomorrow" (Abbé Godin, to the French bishops).

II

"THE DEVELOPMENT of civilized thought can be described as the discovery of identities amid diversity" (Whitehead). Would not this be true of the development of civilized *religious* thought as well? To the point where the civilized (and civilizing) content of religion can be judged against this norm—that it welcomes and encourages diversity of outlook, of expression, of styles of life— and in that degree becomes a worthy reflection of the rich and wild diversity of creation, of the new creation as well as the old? On the other hand, the drawing together of knots of believers into closer and closer flocks, out of the world's cold, can only be construed as a regression, a de-civilizing.

Christ is certainly shepherd; and we are just as certainly not sheep.

The truth of grace, rightly understood, is not merely the *discovery* of identities amid diversity. It is the *creation* of identities amid diversity. The words are crucial, as stated. There is alienation present to the degree that consciousness rejects others who are "different"; and at that point extrapolates itself as ideal or model of perfection. This is precisely the risk of the Incarnation, as it lives on in the faith of believers. Often an Identity is adored, and its implicit Diversity is despised. An incomplete faith, to say the least. Paul insists, by way of contrast, that the Identity only fully reveals itself *in* the diversity; the Head in and through its members: "His own Body."

Is there not a more authentic Christian consciousness present in the minority which is struggling to be recognized without being neutralized or lost in the mass, as contrasted with the "clean" majority which is also struggling, sometimes with the persistence of death itself, to remain immune from all assimilation? Even though this majority prides itself on all the Christian presuppositions: sacraments, tradition, salvation?

Life has very few proofs to offer, of its value, of its necessities, of its very existence. Indeed, the quest for proofs often betrays the presence of second-rate minds. Whereas largeness of understanding is attuned to the necessarily untidy and incoherent aspects that await the ordering mind—and heart.

The search for proofs in the religious sphere implies that some are striving for identity by way of the control of others. The rhetorical mind, proceeding as though the world were a vast meeting hall, in which the prize went to the loudest auctioneers or debaters.

Reality proves very little; it indicates a great deal by way of the epiphany of signs that always accompany mystery, like the influence cast off by radioactive material. Knowledge therefore has all the imprecision of involvement, rather than the "clarity and distinctness" of logic.

The command to the prophet is "eat the book." As though his guts would afterward prove anything about the content of the book!

The parables of Christ were not a tactic aimed at the simple-minded, but an overpouring of divine imagination. Christ would, in any case, not have recast them into a *summa*, given a more learned audience. The parables were at once His way of apprehending creation and God, and His way of communicating with men as men. The purpose of His speech: to create imaginative men, capable of imagining the real world.

—One of the most sorrowful of experiences: encountering religious difficulties unconnected with the real world.

—Some of the most pitiable people: believers unconnected with the world.

—A pitiable religion: not because insecure or under duress or contemned, but because it has grown stale and insipid in its own isolation.

A certain skepticism before answers—prior, apodictic, those offered before the problem has even been posed, those that forbid the problem from presenting itself, those that despise complexity.

Not that approaches to answers are not useful, so long as their tentative, hypothetical nature is taken into account. What is required is the courage to live with questions whose true import is not to be found in answers at all. The clue is in the "signs" that reveal themselves to the listening heart, and so reprove our unmortified tamperings. Such signs lead to further questions, in the nature of things. The road does not reach its end when an "answer" is near; it forks out in two or five or a hundred new directions.

Qualitative faith. A Little Sister of Jesus said, "Our fraternity may have existed only to give one poor woman a flower, and to hear her say, 'This is the first flower I have ever received. . . .'" Kierkegaard says, "If the contemporary generation had left nothing behind but these words: We have believed that in such and such a year, God appeared in our community, and finally died—it would be more than enough."

The fate of the world is my fate. The bridging of that statement, the "passing over," is so vast and perilous, that only Christ can encompass it. Others can throw over hand ropes or beckon one across, but for a stable historical passage to which I can entrust my feet, to which I can entrust those I love, only Christ can be trusted.

Many who call most energetically for change in the Church are among the least informed about the reality of the Church. They really expect the Church to "work" in the way any large corporation is expected to work—or to go out of business. But as a matter of fact, there is no promise given by God that things will go well for us. Nor are our criteria necessarily His. Neither history nor the Bible assure us that the Church will have the vitality or imagination or moral passion to affect human life for the better, in a large perceptible sense. Utopia is not her name. From the point of view of the person anxious for change, refusing to face such hard talk may well mean a refusal of the only promise God has really given us: "In the world you will have suffering."

And what follows: "I have overcome the world." Not by a show of force, even of the icy moral rectitude of the good Pharisee, but by a submission so radiantly pure that it wins all conscience and assumes all hope to itself. There is no other way, as Christian way.

The writer or artist who has had something to say, may, after he has said everything, still have left something undone. The sense of this incompletion may be shattering in proportion as his artistic life has been a personal outpouring, in contrast with an endless window dressing of his own ego.

What is left to do? Some consuming gift of himself which his art, even his art, has left ungiven.

In the midst of much talk of change and renewal, a constant purifying of sources. Prayer, listening, attentiveness to unexpected voices; and, above all, the sense of Christ summoning us to tragedy and to its resolution in the world. Otherwise, we risk wasting our substance upon the latest fashion.

In comparison with the anguish being experienced by many in seeking the merest foothold on the mystery of life, the debates and decrees of churchmen must seem like the planning of a new decor for the old salon. Meantime, the city is burning.

What is needed is to strip the salon, sell the antiques, and throw open the doors to the poor—the Church as house of hospitality to the world.

We are experiencing at present a release of energy (dynamism) that has been gathering force for at least the last century; the labors and thought of anonymous men who articulated the future in spite of great difficulties—legalism, failure of vision, lack of sympathy. They died before the dawn. We must be worthy of a light we did not create, a new church in whose making we have had little or no part. And what a reproof their quality is to our noisiness.

One is permitted skepticism before a call to obedience issued by those who have never paid the cost of an idea, or sweated through its complexities—or announced it with courage.

When the real world, and decisions that make the world recognizable as a moral harmony are in question churchmen are not, in the nature of things, supposed to be ignorant or hostile. Quite the opposite, according to their own sources.

Truth that descends only from the top eventually ceases to flow at all. It becomes glacial or sterile, or both. The free flow is at lower altitudes, where the heat of the day forces men to cast aside their impedimenta, to live in a simpler frame of mind, to speak and share with one another.

A tentative mind requires a long life to embody and express its view of life. Realities recede as they are approached; they must be surrounded and penetrated slowly. Otherwise men send back tourist photos or weather reports on mysteries. Implied here is the tragedy of unusual men who die young. And the tragedy of a fruitful life come to term still too far ahead of its times really to be effective. The saving feature is that other men and other times seize on such lives and put their insights to work. Nothing wasted.

The principle of conservation of matter: nothing wasted. Is this not a "sign" of another harmony, infinitely more complex and mysterious—the conservation of spirit? We shall never know its laws in this world.

The inevitable sadness attached to life in any great city has something to do with the violent, haphazard juxtaposition of extremes which in the countryside have fire breaks or open fields or snow fences between. Rich and poor, black and white, lonely and beset, cynical and broken, suffering and privileged. The witch's brew, poisonous in so many ways, still has the power of fermenting its own antidote.

To let the world in has its price. The mode of selectivity, which is also the only guardian of sanity, is the point here. How much reality? But the question is not a quantum one at all, nor an outward-inward motion. One does not take the world as he takes medicine or dessert. The man who is alive to the real world already contains and expresses it. He *is* the world, at its loftiest epiphany. Rather than a somnolent, drifting sponge on its sea, he is like a pure vessel which pours out on the world its sacred overflow—the spirit which nourishes the world.

Love between two must still include the world.

Love between two, in proportion as it is parasitic, will be abstract and weightless in regard to all others. (The lovers in Dante's hell who are floating and wheeling.)

Love between two, in proportion as it is spiritually incarnate, will be personal and universal when it turns to the world. As indeed it is continually turned.

An ecstasy comparable to that of the flesh is experienced on occasion when the mature man embraces the world.

How many preachers would survive, and for how many sermons, if they were preaching the gospel instead of an apothecary's manual?

How many would stay to hear the sermon out?

Preaching the gospel necessarily implies inclusion of the world, situating the speaker and his hearers mercilessly in its landscape of crime and hope.

There is no political skill equal to the task of "disestablishing" the Church. This is true because her formal establishment in privilege and power is not a matter of political maneuvering at all. We must look rather to her own will—endemic and perennially renewed, always in need of bloody surgery—to attach herself to money and security. The world, the pride of life, live within her. No one imposes sin on her. She herself is sinner.

Teilhard's optimism must strike against the bitter face of experience: "First in life comes joy, then after, sorrow." There is hardly a life which does not bear out the formula. Youth constructs an architecture of ideals, all in its own mind; but one comes to inhabit, toward the end, a shoddy hut—and to go native in it, in a kind of base contentment. A thoughtless, exhausted counterfeit peace, for having at least touched the last mile, and thrown up a shelter there.

Christian suffering—also undergone in the misapprehension of Christ. Does not the Bible place His victory outside time and this world? Why, then, the stubborn, triumphant spirit that keeps issuing invitations to His crowning and enthronement in this world? The meaning of history is not that the Servant advances through stages of indenture, lower bourgeoisie, nobility, to the throne. It is that the Servant is dedicated, while time lasts, to servitude. This is the only permanent form of the Incarnation. So that the last day will not witness the final step in a logical rise of the "son who made good," but the intervention of the Father, against all expectation, all ambition for him, even on the part of Christians. We have something of this insistence on fidelity in the judgment scenes of Matthew: It is the poor, the despised, the undeserving, who cast off their rags at the word of Christ; their identity is finally clear, even to the saved: "the least of these, my brethren." And in their midst, revealed at last, the One who Himself chose "the role of slave."

One cannot become man except in and through the world. One cannot become Christian except in and through the world. Daily and hourly dependence on food, organic life, air, is thus a parable of what is occurring within the spirit. A parable, let it be added, to be stayed with and returned to. Nothing more pitiful than the spirit that has cast its moorings from this humble dependence.

The attrition of life in the world! Only relieved by the hope that the world one lives in is a real world; and that its mysterious elixir "renews the inner man from day to day, even while the outer man is worn down."

To be vindicated by an intervention of God—the last temptation of the valiant. Whereas in fact there is no guarantee of His approval in the way one has both chosen and been chosen for. There is only the value that has summoned, in the light of conscience, with the spiritual greatness of the living and of the dead to lead one on. Any other course of life would be a game of charades played out in a waxworks. Such another course would also blind one to the greatness around him: the men of good will who are also making their way through great perplexity, pain, and anonymity.

Unless one has seen the alternatives to his life, he has never really seen his life.

The wish for further, greater sacrifice—all well and good. But what of the sacrifice demanded here and now? The best gauge of one's grasp on a concrete and possible future (as distinguished from an illusion) is one's grasp on the present.

Fidelity to a vision carries some far ahead of others along the same road. So a man of vision may become a mere ghost or mirage to his friends—too great a distance for communion. One's responsibility, consequently, on any point of the road, is to close or at least lessen the distance between man and man, by a passion for sacrifice and communion. To be near, to intersect, to converge. A star stands, not light-years distant, but in the very eye of him who regards it.

The *anamnesis* of the eucharist is the most powerful and irresistible example of the force of memory among living men. A memory which is an actuality. Memory is a dead force only to those content to live on among the dead. To the living it is a new seed cast in the furrow of the living heart: sacrifice, joy, conquest.

Anamnesis situates us again and again at the core of the Christian issue, which is simply to give one's life, and thereby to find his life. It is in fact the most carnal and concrete of activities. To remember is to eat and drink of a flesh and blood given, poured out "for you." To remember in this way is to become worthy of being remembered—of being eaten and drunk by the unborn.

X—a young priest who is judging life firmly and dispassion-
ately, as a Christian judges. He preaches with care and zeal, gives
himself to the poor, and, beyond his minimal needs, keeps nothing of his income for himself. All the necessary virtues, and in
serene harmony. "What then is lacking to me?" With regard to
the present, nothing. With regard to a whole life—everything;
fiery ordeals, harmony broken, virtues challenged, the reasser-
tion of selfishness, lust, the corrosive attrition of routine, the
contempt of others. In brief, a holiness that has passed through
death to life.

The distinguishing mark of religious action is suffering (Kierkegaard). There is a distinction in order here: action vs. activity.
Religious action comes from the very soul of man; he does not
(literally) lose himself in it; rather, he finds himself. What he
finds is not easily lived with. It must include the immense power
of self-intoxication and illusion and hatred of the truth that
lies in the heart of man. And then, since action terminates in
another person rather than in things or the void, there is a
counterbalance: The judgment "I am guilty" or "I am without
hope" or "I am alone" is modified by the presence of mercy and
innocence and hope. The suffering is not narcotized; it is made
bearable. And this is all the "answer" Christianity can offer.
The Person who is present, available, and merciful.

Activity, on the other hand, starts from without; outside the
agent, and, in an even more terrible sense, outside the world.
Not beginning from within man, it cannot end within him. It
arranges new juxtapositions of events or matter, or manipulates
persons to suit the times, to suit the ego. So it implies no real
suffering at all, in a Christian sense, because Christian suffering
has at least something to do with the discovery of one's being
before God, and before others; at its deepest, the need of grace,
the fact of sin, the possibility of innocence. Activity cannot bring
about this saving sense, which is also a sense of the world, in
living relationship to the living God. Activity can only offer the
emptiness of a life that has discovered, soon or late, not only
that the task was wrongly done, but also that it was wrongly
conceived and begun.

Christian suffering is often undergone most terribly in the apprehension of change. Why am I a stranger to myself? why am I not a moral unity? Can conscience really operate when it must be not the witness or judge of change outside itself, but itself the subject of change? And why this incapacity of spirit, brutally experienced every day? Matter undergoes the world, and so achieves its apotheosis; how can spirit achieve itself apart from the world, from change, and submission? Why does matter always win?

In considering the value of one's life, the real point is not that one is accepted by the living, or even, in anticipation, by the unborn. One acts before God—who is the God of the living as well as of the unborn. He is the God of history. And therefore, in accepting one's witness, He ratifies it as being within history, as He is within history. So one's witness is both on behalf of history, and beckoned beyond it.

It is not enough that man appear to himself as a problem. Still, such a view is a beginning, and the beginning of all real thought. It is the point of division from the world of nature, where problems are only an embolism in a rhythm, imperfections on the wheel of seasons or days—which other seasons and days will restore and renew. But this automatism offers nothing to man's spirit, whose freedom has a horror of solutions from below.

There has never been a skill capable of phrasing "I love you" in a way that could capture the immediate, unique epiphany of another person, here and now realized and radiant. But for consolation: There are other arts at hand. And most effective and befitting of all, that of silence.

The reflective life of man must be balanced by the experience of man, and vice versa. Each taken alone is nearly useless, and possibly ruinous. There is need on the one hand of a break with security, regulation, and reflection, when experience insists on a breakthrough. And there is equally the question of bringing reflective seriousness to bear on one's experience, so that "what happens" does not merely happen, but gets into the guts and soul.

One begins to be a competent specialist by simply living, by being present to experience as an individual, wholly intent on the simple, human, immediate nature of events. Thus, the writer is not among men as writer, but as man; so the artist, the scientist, the saint. Beware of masks, even the most exalted. When special gifts have value in life, they develop out of this will which wants, not to make its mark (or worse, to gather flora for its lab work) but to be present to life; "piety toward experience" is of the essence.

Solitude and community; both must be granted to a man. One is not speaking geographically, but humanly. "It is in solitude that man becomes a question to himself" (Buber). One might add: It is in communal experience that the question loses its icy, impassive, demonic quality, and that if not answered, is at least surrounded with the possibility of being borne with.

In Aristotle, man ceased to be a question, not because he was solved or dissolved in community or in isolation, but because he was posed as an outsider. He was urged by this system to become a kind of dispassionate spectator of himself. The mind considered man from its own self-conscious transcendence, and so made of him a case, a phenomenon. It is clear how such a view of life and of mankind—everything in the third person, myself a "him," the world an "it"—awakens the revulsion of modern men. Today a passionate self-consciousness, and the ironic simultaneity of achievement and of desperate insecurity, make man and his universe into one erect "I," make man a kind of universal exposed nerve and root. You cannot touch creation anywhere without touching him. And this very touchiness is his hope. The Bomb, created by his own hands, is finally seen in its lurid and true light. It is wielded, that is, against himself.

One thinks often of those who suffer, and most of all of good men who suffer. And one is appalled, because he himself does not suffer. Almost as though he had heard the iron corollary: "Of what good are you . . . ?" Until one reaches a further depth, and the sense that to suffer or not to suffer are indifferent things. The only thing is fidelity to the moment, to those one loves or is required to love. It does not matter greatly that such fidelity does not cost greatly, for the moment. What matters is that the fidelity is present, and radiantly so. The cost will appear.

Suffering often takes the most personally humiliating and opaque character. It incapacitates a man from the very good which was the cause of his greatness in the first place. He can no longer act with that spontaneity and clarity which had so won others. He is now thrown upon the mercy of others, a burden to them; more, he is bewildered and unable to give an account of himself. He cannot explain why or how he suffers; even though once he could reveal, winningly and joyfully, why life took the shape it did, why it was right and fitting that it did so. The scandal of such suffering, suffering that plucks the tongue from the head and the voice from the heart! even to the point that others are scandalized and bewildered. They had concluded over the years that whatever came to pass this man would never cease to be their oracle; the years would only confer on him a clearer, more communicable wisdom. But to be reduced to a deaf mute?

Cui bono? Man does not suffer that a world may be one; he does not suffer, even, that the will of God may be accomplished. He is, in fact, in the deepest suffering, evacuated of all real purpose at all. He is not suffering "in order that." His anguish does not allow him to be carried beyond the fact of suffering. And this is true so that the truth of suffering, its value as sign, may shine forth. But only for the few who are ready to read such a sign. Achievements, great moments, visible accomplishments, always have about them so much danger of distraction, egoism, ambiguity. But the sufferer who believes and takes his stand, not precisely on his suffering, nor on the quality of his faith, nor on the "good" he is doing, nor on the response of his friends, but on Christ alone; which is to say, on the living truth of things —this man, perhaps for the first time, has become a true sign. He is the sign of the cross. There is quite possibly no other in the world today.

III

To OPEN one's life more and more to the possibilities of the *magis*. But the true limits of the *magis* cannot be known unless one tries the door and searches out the boundaries. Freedom is not living on as a prisoner who has demanded (and even possibly won) greater privileges. And the barriers, even though set by a most determined and stern unfreedom in others, are not ultimately erected by others at all. They are the forms that personal cowardice has allowed, the forms of slavery that one's own life has permitted.

Every question left unanswered or equivocated by the living, appears in the next generation as an iron necessity. But a few men in every generation have the power to break the slaveries that the past has accumulated. We call such men saviors, and we are right.

A fact that strikes us when we have the courage to look at the prophets and the life they led, is that such men often stood outside the community. They were often excommunicated; at least one can say that their words were hardly ever a part of an accepted canon. Only time and reflection help us to rehabilitate them, to confess that they stood all the while in the mainstream of God's historic enterprise. Their hope was His. But who will rehabilitate us?

The rejection of the prophets must always be seen at its deepest, as the attempt (often undertaken by religious men) to banish God from history. God cannot be stomached, or if He can be, it is only after he has been "processed" into a pablum for infants. St. Paul indeed recognized an acceptable infancy period. But hardly as a permanent arrangement for the fullness of time.

Le trahison des clercs takes place today when intellectuals dedicate themselves to organizational good-housekeeping rather than to world need. Such men actually pull down the dwelling

32

they purpose to support; they fumigate it of all vestiges of the Holy Spirit.

A sign of clerical maturity is a growing uneasiness with the task of overcontrol of consciences. Such control has traditionally operated within suspiciously narrow boundaries. One was not introducing other lives to a vision of reality so much as to a program controlled by clerics, and forming lay enclaves of further control. The theme was a predictably Pharasaic one: *Be like us!* But it led to a dead end, to slavery rather than to Christ's infinite freedom. Auricular confession has often represented a kind of apogee of this activity. One individual met another in darkness and secrecy, with no chance to stand with men, conscious of guilt against them and seeking restoration to them. It was not often apparent in such a method that guilt against God had taken a concrete historic form, if indeed the guilt was a genuine one. Or that forgiveness should be as dramatic and evident as genuine guilt.

Satan's works are always epiphanies; it is only Christ who dares to disappear in the world.

Our deepest fear is to be doomed to disappearance; as is so often true, the fear is the other face of the summons.

Fanaticism differs from concern not because the former is impassioned or single-minded, but because it is autochthonous. It cannot ray out in organized conscience, or see an issue in its landscape—a faculty which is both a source of mercy and of instruction. A man of concern can live in the human landscape, even when it is bestial or abandoned. But the fanatic can only further ravage it.

A man is first in trouble not when authority reacts to his activity, but when he himself first acts freely. So to act, given our world, is strictly illegal—it is picking the lock on one's own jail.

Moral recoiling from every form of violence, if it is to be responsible, must avoid the paralysis that results from too intemperate a sense of horror. Our emotional life must be *useful* —to ourselves and others. Granted the real world is vicious and terrifying in many ways. But it is always bearable. A moral sense must submit to formation by the real; to the admission that nothing is too big, too real, too unreal to be lived with. Man is made for the world, even for our world. It is doubtful that he can come to maturity apart from the terrifying realities that surround him. Unless this is admitted, moral activity ends in the madhouse, or in the intramural childishness which is another form of treason. A real question for real men—What light can you shed? Woe to the high-minded, over-fastidious man who merely pours darkness upon darkness.

An act of faith in the form one's life has actually taken does not preclude a continuing critique upon that form of life—quite the contrary. Indeed, the function of love of life is the unwillingness to allow a creeping tyranny of the unconscious or of history to assume control over conscious life—a life which in principle cannot bear with the prospect of shrinking alternatives.

Religion in the service of war—a more complete debasement of a life form is hardly imaginable. Such debasement is also quite universal.

The books of the New Testament, with their consistent tone of freshness, virile resistance to evil, their call to a new aeon, their promise of new resources to meet new crises. On the other hand, man does not easily renounce his biology, his inheritance of evil and hatred, his fascination with games of destruction. It is so often true, even today, that old hands take up the new Book. And since evil seeks the sanction of holiness, men also take up the pen—to rewrite the Book which in its plain text is unbearable. It *must* be possible to resist evil with evil, to kill the innocent, to wage war on mankind, to deflect the divine promise of plenty in the direction of nuclear security. When such thinking is generally accepted by religious men, a very simple and evil thing has happened. The sacred books have not intervened at all. History goes forward precisely as though such books had never been written, as though religious men had never existed.

It is possible only to the most gifted and integral conscience to draw implications from moral principles. Or to sense the symbolic nature of present action—so that literally every moral choice exerts a summons toward a further heroism. In such a way, the nonviolent implications of the civil rights movement prepared men for peacemaking everywhere in the world.

When moral outrages are perpetuated near at hand, they awaken an instinctive reaction. Who, provided he is human, can see a Negro beaten without responding? But distance enchants: What man sees Vietnamese peasants brutalized, and responds to that?

The moral energy of mature men requires an operating circumference as large as the universe. Otherwise their energies burn out for want of a field of force.

The critique upon religious history offered with free-wheeling crudeness (as by Bertrand Russell) or with fastidious intelligence (as by Santayana) or with nearly total ignorance (by the average man today) offers at least a new chance to thoughtful men of faith—the chance of humility, the revaluation of their claims.

An exalted and pure form of renouncement: the longing that those whom one loves and values be not submitted to needless suffering. The sense of waste is exacerbated by love of life. On the other hand, indifference to suffering, ignorance of the value of those who suffer, closes the gap until literally anything is bearable. But what can close the wound opened between value and suffering? Only a greater love—only, perhaps, suffering itself.

If a policy of violence wins out on a given occasion, the way of nonviolence is again proven wrong—thus the judgment of the violent. The policy of nonviolence must admit the historic fact of successful violence; which is to say that nonviolence cannot look to human outcomes for its justification.

One does not judge reality by its degree of rigor and difficulty. Life may possibly be tranquil and joyous. But it probably will not be, and one had best be prepared.

Modesty of outlook. Neither true evil nor true good admit of rhetoric. The former is rendered modest by its achievements in history, the latter by a sense of its precarious, tolerated existence; both by a wisdom which knows that good and evil are inseparable in this world.

Imaginary love plays fancy footwork round a moment that never arrives. Incarnate love lives in the moment, and pays the price.

The remedy against romantic love: "Pay to God and to the neighbor the minimum which justice exacts here and now" (Weil). In such a way the minimum may even become an acceptable form of love.

The passions of men are ordered to the love of God. But they do not love God in fact; they love Him only by transvaluation; that is, the passions must be drawn and taught to love God, with endless patience and discretion. Otherwise they only succeed in aping or debasing love.

The analogies of faith lead irresistibly to the world and to time. To deny these analogies, to argue from the holy to the holy for vindication of the holy is increasingly useless. When one makes his act of faith, and then stands determinedly with men, with conscience, for the liberation of the oppressed, then his argument takes on flesh. One may possibly be human by determining to be Christian.

The historic sin of Christians: overcontrol of others. The historic reparation: modesty, anonymity, service.

By a violent determination to "appear"—that is, to win out— Christianity actually disappears in history. Christianity first truly appeared as an expression of God's hope for man—which is to say, by a deliberate disappearance—in " serving, not being served."

An imaginary god will always demand an epiphany, a forced presence, a mounting of the battlements—as a god of war. The true God takes no clear form in the soul, or in history. He remains a mystery, as the first consequence of His existing at all.

Every great end imperfectly or impurely conceived allows the freest play to man's base inclinations. In the name of God, and for His honor, anything is allowable—the tactic of Renaissance Christendom. But every great end perfectly and purely conceived purifies its own means.

The hardest task for believing men who are dedicated to their world is not the task of justifying themselves before the world. It is the task of justifying themselves before the Church.

Priests are not truly open to death—in their consent, their refusals, their words and silence, their intelligence and imagination. Hence their incapacity for life, and their feeble contribution to life.

To live by the values of a structure is to exist without a soul; it is a life in death which offers only the feeblest energy to the unborn; it is the dissolution of a cloud overhead. No charge, no thunderclap, no healing rain.

In proportion as one is more open to divine influence, he is more open to diabolic influence. The need for discernment of spirits. But the spirits will never be discerned by neutrals, that is by those to whom all spirits are indifferent.

"But why do you endanger the causes you work for by entering into *this*—the most despised and neglected and obscure of all?" Because the truth of one's life is put in question by the presence of this one need. One cannot offer a piecemeal conscience to life.

The futility of confronting with a vision of life minds ruled by slogans. Which cannot mean that communion is impossible —only that it is terribly difficult.

To cherish inwardness of spirit, possessed and possessing; and to keep at distance the powers that claim possession. A possession by the Holy Spirit is indivisible and total. A vacuum of soul, on the other hand, invites in "seven devils" and the last state of that man is worse than the first.

Sometimes, by an intolerable pretension, the unjust are restrained from killing, under the illusion that their malice will give a martyr to history. Which of course such men can never do. The best they can do is to act as the slaves of destiny, to set and light the stage of tragic victory, to manipulate its scenery, to draw the curtain and to close it.

It is only in the effort to turn toward others in love that one is given self-knowledge—both of his goodness and of his evil. But supposing unawareness and indifference are a state of death, what a resurrection this effort supposes! It is quite possibly a form of Christ's resurrection in this world.

One's evil known clearly and even unbearably; one's goodness known obscurely or not at all. Is this not the exact state of supernatural hope?

Only those who love life are deserving of life. A sense of outrage against violations of life fills one, not with a craven longing for death, but with a new determination to see life vindicated. Blessed are the peacemakers. Our handiwork in Vietnam and Hiroshima should, if we are worthy of life at all, create a new race, however small, of purified gift-givers, men who make up for the death-dealing of many and the indifference of most.

The meaning of courage: neither a vapid excessive energy, nor the will to dominate experience. At its best, a free submission—to person, to community.

"The tree of sin is truly a tree; while the tree of life is a stick in the ground, something which offers no fruits, but simply expresses a vertical movement. One can kill vital energies in himself in order to preserve only his vertical movement. Flowers and fruits are even a waste of energy if one wishes solely to attain the heights" (Weil).

In times of deepest interior trouble, the world seems to break up like an exposed shack in high winds. Nothing is substantial any more. But the highest achievement still remains possible in such times, perhaps in the obscure understanding that something real is at last at hand. One has gotten beyond the false impermeability of all that formerly seemed necessary and real. To touch bottom, to touch height? The words are not helpful. One is, and things around are not. And meantime one is free to see and describe what lies beyond the present chaos, and what must be endured within it.

The benefit of precept is not to form a man according to the law. It is to form a man of freedom—another matter entirely. The precepts have a certain directive validity for man. But the man who stays under them for their own sake dies of suffocation.

The symbol which Lent brings home: "A blind man, a beggar, stood by the road." Blind in apprehension of beauty and goodness —but not totally deprived of channels of life. He heard and spoke and was healed. And he was a beggar; in the face of such an image, who can claim possession of the poor of the Kingdom? We live in shrouds.

The state of sin is ultimately the incapacity of man to know himself as sinner; here, he is Pharisee; hereafter, he is the damned.

The Gospels are always behind the times—but only because Christians are reading them.

The imaginative horizon of Christ: not to shun the "analogies from beneath." "Think of the wild flowers, how they neither work nor weave." Not to be afraid of this humility, even though our fear and cowardice go so far as to forget the analogies from above.

One does well to celebrate intelligence in the service of faith. But what of the corruption of intelligence in the service of the law?

One does not first go to the law in order to improve the law —nor to canon lawyers in order to renew the Church. In the one case, disciplined public protest is first required. In the second, a return to roots, which involves also a protest against unjust law, even unto death.

At certain periods, men find themselves alone, without experts, without intellectuals, without religious visionaries, in the front lines of the world's questions. And this is a terrible thing. The deprived are forced to take the lead because somehow, somewhere along the way, the wise and great and gifted have fumbled. They are simply not at man's side. If they arrive at all, they come late, impelled by a conscience which their disciplines have hardly allowed to awaken. But this is the glory of man and an irony of God: While intelligent men falter, a few unexpected men win the day without them. Such men, neither first-rate minds nor engineers of world change, nevertheless forged in a few years, and even in a few days, new instruments of change. Such men created themselves. And the outside, inert world has been forced to admiration of social movements that could not tarry until the scholarship and competence which were so desperately needed would consent to catch up. In facing the present with courage, a few men create their own future. A future, one must insist, which the belated experts have had no real grasp on, a vision they could not communicate to those who place their faith in cautious wisdom and rational timepieces.

What is in question today is a new grasp on time itself. And even more deeply, a new conception of the possibility of spirit. When all has been said, it is the liberals who have lost all practical, viable confidence in the power of spirit to effect spiritual change; which is to say, in the power of spirit simply to be itself. And it is the poor, the depressed, who are shown to be the guardians of existence.

The temptation of the alienated liberal: to take up useless arms, to imprison spirit in matter, as a child is encumbered by the warrior's mailed armor. Not incarnation, but immobilization.

When the spirit grows weary of being spirit, it seeks to inhabit the houses of the powerful, to take their tools in hand, to qualify a vocation which has grown intolerable with the "limiting factors" of life in the world. Which is not so much an incarnation as the takeover of man by the principalities and powers.

How can I become human? The question can always be posed in outer space. There, it is of course unanswerable. Nothing to grasp, nothing to pay. Weightlessness, a void.

Real questions demand a context; the mystery of other lives. Only a neighbor can answer—by another question which his very presence raises, How much will you pay to be human?

The religious life is in many ways another blockage against real answers to real questions. Systematized theology replaces life. Abstract answers are given to paper questions. One begins with the inheritors of the faith, reduces the possibilities of doubt to a minimum, and forbids risk. Out of this favored ingrowth *may* emerge a remnant who decide in favor of the world, of history, of social dedication. Meantime, the Unitarians, the Quakers, begin at the opposite side, with a remnant whose presence and action had raised questions already. They start in a human landscape, with small service groups, and awakened consciousness. Out of this *may* arise a community of conscience. The risk is real and part of the process.

Communion with a neighbor at my side, in the ditch, in jail, *may* arouse imagination to the point where the absent neighbor becomes real. In such a way, many become peacemakers because civil rights have become a real and present issue. Conversely, the indifferent liberal easily bears with the pushbutton war dance.

"Let us suppose that certain individuals resolve that they will consistently oppose to power the force of example; to authority, exaltation; to insult, friendly reasoning; to trickery, simple honor. Such men would indeed be preparing for the future. Who can fail to see the positively dazzling realism of such behavior?" (Camus)

Every step in a real direction enlarges one's identity, providing only he has not cheated by omitting a prior step. But what does this mean? Who or what is to measure degrees of unfreedom? Is the analogy useful indeed at all—the analogy of childhood and manhood, of baby steps and giant steps? Say rather, that one was ignorant and innocent as a stone. Now he is breathed upon; now he knows his ignorance.

The abstract mind, whether it be clerical, lay, or secularist, is profoundly at one in its inanition. It is invariably unmarked by respect for the healing nature of revolution. So it invariably acts as mortician or trifler—after the fact, approving what has passed, unable in principle to get into the mainstream. Our example is drawn from today. Four or five years after the event, when picketing is becoming less effective as a means of redress, men accept picketing. The institution has again canonized the dead. But the least and mildest threat to inconvenience of the normal lives of those in possession—by sit-ins, or traffic blockage —becomes a new form of scandal.

After a moral crisis it is impossible not to be bettered or worsened. But the greatest loss of all is the loss of communication. Possibility: the clearing of the air, a new look at issues; at its deepest, an inkling of who we are and of where we are to go.

The cross of Christ is, practically speaking, the blindness and vanity of men. Not as welcomed and lived by the oppressor. But inflicted and passed on—to the innocent. The guilty cannot bear the cross; so they lay it on other shoulders.

From the possession of one correct idea, firmly in place, firmly in relation with other ideas, what great things can be expected! Especially when we consider that good men ordinarily operate from incorrect or unassimilated or inferior ideas. And that the majority of men live for long periods rather completely untouched by any ideas.

To put on the universe as another body. Or to put on the

Body of Christ as another (and the only) Body. One and the same investing.

One cannot start as pure man to live in the world. The true beginning is as impure man—in order to become pure man, in and through the world.

"What does our faith tell us to do when the world does not listen to us? It tells us that we are not responsible for turning history out right—but that we *are* responsible to be where we should be when history does turn out right. 'Blessed are those servants who are vigilant'—in suffering and in servanthood" (Yoder).

The Church of Christ is the only "normal" church. Which is to say, her special competence is for abnormal times. And in normal times (which are invariably worldly times) the Church induces crises, rather than acting as oil on the waters.

An ecumenism that includes the world.

The work of the principalities and powers includes a closure against alternatives. We are left only a gross, Neanderthal minimum; which is to say, destruction vs. survival. The work of the spirit includes openness, suppleness, vast and imaginative alternatives, issuing from a firm center.

One cannot be forbidden to be a human being, even in the name of God. The difficulty is that "being human" is so unfamiliar a task that the efforts toward it are in the nature of things shocking. The social amassing of brains and money and power in an inhuman direction is an enormous inhibition. One becomes inhuman by following the general road, well marked and well guarded. One becomes human today only by protest, as the Negro has shown us. There are no military carriers, no aerial maps to show this way, to bear one toward it. "Come into a land which *I* will show you."

What is required of a prophet is not to arouse the passions of men, but to awaken the nascent passion of true intelligence.

The existence of all men requires the suffering of all men to sustain it. In this sense, Christ is already included, as one man in an anonymous mankind.

But guilt requires innocence to make the sufferings of the guilty acceptable or bearable, or indeed to grant the guilty any meaning at all. In this sense Christ introduces Himself to His own race as the stranger who, by his stupendous act of freely choosing love, has become the friend.

The acts of God are unimaginable and personal, or, as the Bible says, "jealous." I cannot imagine my own conversion, any more than I can enact it.

Christianity started small—and keeps getting smaller. The great fact is not the mustard tree in which the birds of the air dwell. It is the dropping of seeds—each one throughout history miraculously like the other, the last like the first in the furrow of time.

We must grant many defects of love to those who are in love. We must grant many deficiencies in truth to those who love the truth.

The cross in its deepest meaning is not experienced when we relive the tragic externals, even in the highest form of witness, which is martyrdom. Mystery means inwardness—the rest is accidental. What really counts is a life which may or may not have a tragic ending, but which is lived under a sign of submission and of freedom.

We must have recourse to something beyond depth psychology to understand what we are experiencing in these days. The principalities and powers—nothing merely human could explain the grip that violence has on men, the massive, unshakable triviality of the majority, the silence of men who hold responsibility for us, the bombers that go out each day in spite of con-

science and of world opinion, the evidence of torture, the Algerian
and German experience, lived over in a kind of witless blindness.
The churches have nothing to say; those who speak are silenced.
Is it in such preliminaries that the Householder returns?

Must we see mankind disappear in order to realize at last that
we have never known the reality of the human? Or that the
reality indeed had no meaning for us at all?

The "normalizing" of faith by normal times into a mere
intellectual assent can only be considered as a curse of God.
Faith is abnormal, in the sense that it acts most truly in crisis
and dislocation; it needs unusual times in order that men may
come to faith at all. Otherwise we are left with the good church-
goers of Mauriac who take their religion as they take their
vitamins.

The values one is prepared to die for must become the risks
one is willing to live for. In such a way peacemaking justifies itself
in social responsibility. Indeed, martyrdom can become an obsession and an evasion, as is seen in those believers who flee the
present crisis in the name of God—a God who presumably had
called them *toward*, not out of, their societies.

IV

THE BEGINNING and the middle are defined by the end. If the
end is to remain pure, the middle and beginning must be kept
free of impurities. The great means that determine the purity
of the end are always forms of suffering.

Life often strikes hardest at those who have come through
long failure into success. How sad to see a man live too long to
be allowed to die burdened by real questions!

When we protest war, we cannot be held to account for not
producing an alternative diplomacy. In question here is a "guts"
morality that declares: I cannot bear with this; I stand and protest here. Nothing more can rightly be demanded of Christians.

White men pose the question of Negro identity: "How can an animal metamorphose into a human?" But the Negro knows better, being sure of one thing, his own humanity; and being unsure of another thing—the white man's humanity. And in both cases the Negro is right.

Let us imagine a Negro woman, married to a white man, the mother of his children, standing at the altar to offer the Eucharist. Behold the end, at one stroke, of prejudices that history has reinforced, even in the church—prejudice against women, against blackness, against marriage, against interracial love. A call from the Holy Spirit might some day sound in such a way. After it had sounded, it could never be ignored again.

To put a sting in spontaneous human joy, to introduce suspicion of instinctual life, to substitute the law for the prophets —the perennial vocation of the Pharisee, perennially at large.

Wasted seed, wasted words. But the infinitesimal portion which germinates, which is heard, brings about the most improbable of effects—the renewal of life.

Our happiness is not linked to innocence. It is linked to guilt, and we must bear with this. To link happiness to innocence is to concoct a "better world" than the one God has created.

One must have his back to the wall or stand at the abyss, before he can sense in any real way the limits of his life, the harsh *ne tangas* that surrounds and presses on us; from illness, from sin, from death, from the structures of religion even. The pressures are as impalpable as air, and as killing as air under pressure. But they tell us who we are—men summoned by a merciless act of love. And such pressures prevent our losing our identity in Promethean dreams.

What is to save us from the powers and dominations which Paul saw operating under both Jewish ordinances and Gentile law and order—a double slavery, the organizing of life at the expense of God? The difficulty is a real and continuing one.

Within religious life, the rule falls under the subjection of powers hostile to God whenever it replaces the will of God with "human traditions" (Col. 2: 8). Human traditions seem always to lurk at the edge of the most radiant triumphs of spirit, ready to claim and control the spontaneous truth which has somehow emerged.

The only recourse possible in such a situation is to the *sensus ecclesiae*, which Paul identifies with the sacred overflow of the risen Christ. Such a sense alone discerns the spirits, evil and good. It is pure freedom. It arises in those desert springs of intelligence and love, constantly springing up, even in the jungles and foul alleyways of modern life. In this life, slavery in high places had decreed universal slavery in its own image. But it could not implement its decree. There were not police enough, or the machinery broke down, or someone—even one person—when a chink of light fell on the earth, rejoiced in the realization of the end of night.

Does a movement of order in the world ever occur without a movement of disorder within men? We pay dearly for our social movements, even the most altruistic and unconstrained. Just as we pay dearly for the false peace declared in the compounds of the affluent, in ignorance and indifference of the disorder with which selfishness corrupts our atmosphere.

Infidelity: to indulge the hope of creating public order as the way of evading one's inner disorder. A like infidelity: to stand guard over one's inner order, to fear the "casting off into the deep" implicit in a vocation to public order. The first is an evasion; the second, a slavery.

But who can break the slavery, by way of the truth of fidelity? Who will create a man, vulnerable before the universe, without cheap victimhood or cheap safety? Christ our Lord, in dying, created His destiny—which is precisely to live and to bestow life.

Along the shore after the storm a detritus is cast up. Wrack, dead seaweed, the inflated bags of the Portuguese men-of-war—

their vicious antennae withered to rotten string. A single blow explodes the principalities and powers—a hardened sac of air, a puff of venom, nothing more. But within the sea, out of our element, what a malevolent, invisible threat. Only the Lord walks these waters, and the few men of faith, without being destroyed.

To live in hope, one must have touched the outer limits of personal and public despair. To see that despair has a limit, and to go beyond it.

The great Lenten themes of life and death. Blessed is the man who hears them sounded in Scripture and verified within life—who hears them verified in Scripture because they have sounded in his life.

A raising from the dead far more literal than the one granted the widow's son or the daughter of Jairus. When a man passes from egoism, cliches, propaganda, fear, violence, into a life that places its stake in the Power which has summoned. He knows the stench of death in casting it off.

The openness and fleshly availability of Christ. He can be touched but He cannot be absorbed or corrupted, even by His own. So in the Church He is our hope. He is stranger to no man; but He cannot be made hostage to our unbelief. Not because of what He rejects, but because of what He is, of the way He includes "even the least of us."

The *we* of Christianity always joins hands with the *they* of the world—without its becoming a gentleman's agreement or a Rotarian dream. Firmness and suppleness, an *against* that is also a profound juncture.

"I fancy I know the lesson of living and dying unviolently, and I have yet to demonstrate it by one perfect act" (Gandhi).

If we were to perform our liturgy as it should be performed, we would need less worship. Or rather, all of life would appear for what it is—a continuous worship, a service of God and man. Being dedicated to imperfection, distrustful of mankind, and intent on ourselves instead of one another, we multiply and propagate imperfection as a way of life. Thus, what goes on at the altar appears as the fine point of our conduct within life— impervious, alienated, discontinuous. So do the Mysteries become conundrums.

Objects of compassion:

1. Lives, even intelligent lives, whose enthusiasms have never reached their hour. A dedication to an idea that has progressively contracted; its center in time becomes an obsession instead of a point of departure or a source of communion. Such lives grow increasingly querulous and unhappy. Other men, even the best of them, whose ideas have struck fire, are branded as success mongers; purity of conscience in public is dismissed as a dream.

2. Lives, even dedicated lives, which have passed from a revolutionary fervor, a prophetic fire, into the establishment. From the heights of the establishment, such men now pass judgment on the revolution. If old age is granted, what a gift to die youthful nonetheless! So a long life may be a crown on life instead of a curse, as the prophets realized.

As one's understanding grows, so do one's faults. One cannot face without shame others who look for something from him. In such humiliation a man knows only—and it is a kind of carrion comfort—that he is being emptied of his clericalism and moral pride.

Some men could never be housebroken in debased human dwellings. Such men alone deserve the name servant of the Mystery. They alone have embraced its final outer reaches; they alone will not have God seized upon by human hands.

Suffering becomes useless and destructive when it has no source in the universe, no relationship to the world of man's spirit. A pure inner chaos, a battle among captive animals.

To be explored: the educating power of action, when mighty

currents of conflict are crossing, and in their circuit are raising some men to life and destroying others.

The way religion creates faces in the bureaucratic model. The way faith creates faces in the biblical model.

Is this despair or the desire of God? To yearn at times that there might have been no "religious history" at all for man; no automatic inheritance, no cultural barnacles and taboos, no self-perpetuating lures, no contempt for man. To wish that everyone could be born at the base of Matterhorn, with only one way open to him—up.

"Willy-nilly, actively or passively, one must await the given time; one cannot skip a single moment" (Rosenzweig). The pressure of world change on the Church; something is near which is still outside, which must be responded to. The general principles of human justice may have been enunciated by churchmen, but other men have activated them, without the Church, even perhaps without faith. Will the Church have the unselfish capacity to *receive,* to be enriched by time and this world? There is a *yes* to be said, an anonymous fellowship to be created, a mankind to be ministered to. There are no structures of mercy or justice ready for the task—they must be created as we go along. Will the Church hear a sound which has not been struck from her own towers, but which nevertheless announces a fullness of time decreed by the Savior—Who has not named Himself Savior of the Church only, but also Savior of the World? Will the Church be saved apart from the world which "God so loved"?

In our universal war atmosphere, which certainly implies a kind of madness, it becomes rarer and rarer to find a man who has retained even the aspect of sanity that was fairly common twenty years ago. At that time, your "average good Christian" would have recoiled in horror at war planning that looked cruelly to the destruction of millions of people. Such thinking, he would have declared, belonged to horror fiction, or was traced only on the drawing boards of the enemy. Yet now it is we who are winning the arms race. Our death preparation lumps together an overkill potential that could be actuated in a few minutes to "trade cities" with the enemy. And very few resist. Church conscience takes the easy way down the slope—along with other men. The disappearance of protest, the narrowing of alternatives, is practically universal. The horizon supposedly granted by faith simply is no longer apparent. All men judge and dread the future according to the iron norms established by the military, which today occupies the eschatological throne once claimed, we said, by God alone. The lion has swallowed the lamb. The lion now rules the world; the figure of sacrifice, prophecy, and judgment has been eliminated. Our sacred bestiary can do without Him; He is indeed extinct. Are we facing the rule of the principalities and powers who have presumed to seize the end of things to themselves, to dethrone Him who alone knows the day and the hour of judgment? It is very hard not to think so in the face of the daily news.

"The men of Nineveh feasted and married." What strikes one is the horrifying normalcy of life today, emptied of moral dread and helpless to take up arms against the sea. Meantime, a judgment hangs over us. But the pace of routine is so devouring, men are so horrendously *within* the city, that no one thinks a breakthrough feasible or even possible. Parish life, university life, the normal occupations of all, continue. Men plan for a future, a future that may never arrive. And even if it does, it will certainly have no resemblance to the selfishness and securities we once knew.

We wanted to widen the debate, so that responsible men might be encouraged to speak, and the energies symbolized in religion, art, and intellectual life might be encouraged and released. We wanted to insist that man's conscience had something to say, and we wanted to say it; not to leave the decision of man's survival to those least equipped to bear it—to the military and the power politicians.
We wanted to return to the Gospel without primitivism, to insist that a few key ideas had proved themselves in history, to bring those ideas to bear on the present impasse, which was no more than a larger, more brutal form of a constant impasse, in-

volving contempt for the innocent, idolatry of power, the death of compassion.

We wanted the long view over the short view; we wanted patience to enter the present; we worked to inject hope into man's being.

We succeeded here and now. Men who live the life of the mind and heart spoke up after we had spoken up. Their speech reached as far as the bomb bay and the trigger. They gave us a few moments more in which to begin to talk to others, to begin to trust others.

We insisted that conscience and compassion are invisible. We said this to Negroes wherever we could, knowing that they were best able to hear us. We suggested that in history the man of hope has always been the underdog. But as long as he remained undefeated, he might still save others when the men of power were busy gathering more power and in the process were destroying others. We wished to suggest that the struggle in Alabama was only a preliminary, that the Negro was summoned further—he must protest brutality, and the bombing in Viet Nam, in the Congo, in South Africa. The Negro would never be a man until his voice was heard in all the world. In so speaking, the Negro might even be the first American of all; black as he was, despised and disinherited at home, a suffering servant, "the light of the nations."

"We are called to live in the world as if God did not exist" (Bonhoeffer).

"The Christian is one who lives in such a way that life makes no sense if God does not exist" (Suhard).

How bridge this gap?

Each man does, in his own way. Each of these two died in his own way—the Cardinal with his anguish, the Protestant as martyr. The life of each is comprehensible only because God exists—because He confers on man moral radiance, freedom from fear, heroism in solitude.

Yet each man lived and died as though God did not exist. In this sense—God did not intervene. Hitler flourished; France remained pagan.

To believe in the way these men believed is (1) to be possessed by the living God, and (2) to be freed from the longing for "cheap grace"—idolatrous intervention, miracles of neat human arrangement.

"The good is victorious, but not in time" (Kierkegaard).

What we were trying to do was precisely to give men hope. Our certainty about our task was not a Cartesian clarity. Indeed, we might be wrong; there was a good chance that we were wrong, as our critics both inside and outside the Church did not hesitate to remind us. But there was also a large chance that we were right, and that *they* were wrong. Our chance was based on universality and compassion, and on a striking historical theorem that is as cruel and inevitable as war itself. It declares that *war preparations beget war*. And today we have little time left—preparation for war could quite possibly be the first act of the final war.

The asceticism, the *disciplina arcana* of the early Church, or of the Church at any period, prepares and purifies the act of faith by which a man declares his obedience to Jesus Christ, dead and risen, present and immanent in the universe. Moral life, law, Church forms, take their start here; indeed, they cannot begin anywhere else. Thus the act of faith declares its amplitude and casts off its substitutes and false starts at one blow.

The moral life of Jesus has its roots in the religious life of Jesus. How was His consciousness present to the Father and mankind? A moral stance grew naturally from a sense of existence. But never, for Him or for us, vice versa.

At times, the sublime imagination of Jesus seems to lead us astray. Does He really mean, as Luke seems to indicate, that we are to learn from the lilies and ravens the complexities of a providence which He connects with the cycles of lower nature? "Set your heart on his kingdom, and your food and drink will come as a matter of course" (Luke 12 : 25). But how many men could respond, in eastern Europe or South Africa or in the southern United States today: We have set our hearts on the kingdom, and we have won only concentration camps, starvation, genocide, apartheid, fire hoses, tear gas.

Recourse to the analogy of faith, as commonly understood, a balancing of text against text, is of little help. The doctrine of providence comes easily to the lips of those in possession. But what of "the fate of the majority of men"? (Pope John) The only helpful analogy in this matter is the Christian belief in a profound derangement of divine goodness by human malice; which is to say, an understanding of the omnipresence and the near-omnipotence of evil.

Thus, a certain usefulness of nature is made clear—and the Gospels are set free of a literalism that can hold firm only in a primitive, untroubled bucolic society, such a society being verifiable chiefly in the dreams of those to whom complexity and evil are strangers. But the public life of Christ was lived in an evil society—declared so by His words and overcome in His blood. So His doctrine of "analogy through flora" is balanced by His experience of "analogy in evil." The final balance is His death. Evil had sought to possess even Him, and to corrupt His transcendent message into a political or a legalistic—religious salvation. But He died, and rose again.

Perhaps some evils are so powerful and permeating that victimhood is the only argument against them. One dies without a protest, except his own blood. Nuclear warfare and genocide and racism are the present forms of such evils—today's "principalities and powers and rulers of the upper air."

The function of intellectual discipline is not to dissipate or complicate conscience. It is to concentrate it. Logically, the first man to the block, or on the picket line, or to prison in social crisis, ought to be the intellectual. That he is not first is a treason against the first power of man—his intelligence.

When the believing intelligence is in question, the first man in the enterprises spoken of above ought to be the theologian. When he is not present, one can only speak of a more grievous betrayal—that of the *fides quaerens intellectum.*

The "spiritual gospel" of St. John was discredited by the nineteenth century, for the same reason that the whole Bible is despised by the twentieth century. Neither period can bring a complete vision of man to the reading of the text. Nor are we speaking of a philosophical problem; the difficulty is a matter of conscience, a corruption of the heart. The nineteenth century could live at peace with colonial Africa and the slave trade. The twentieth century lives at peace with Hiroshima and racism. Which is to say that the activity of both centuries renders man illiterate from the point of view of existence. The Gospel simply was not written with such men in mind—except as a judgment upon them.

A sense of discrimination governs one's activity, even the most compassionate, so that the symbolic radiance of one's action is not destroyed; so that the underlying mystery may appear. So Jesus did not heal all the ills of this world, because to heal them all would be to leave the deeper illness both undiagnosed and untouched. It would be to act, not as redeemer but as magic man.

Injustice cannot of itself produce martyrs. It can only produce the damned, in its own image. Only justice itself, lived and suffered for, produces martyrs. This is not to deny that injustice is often the atmosphere and occasion of martyrdom; it forges the sword and raises the gallows. Nevertheless, only faith can give a man to the executioner.

Our situation is a great deal like the Algerian war; priests then were silenced, and even (since the French are less churchy than ourselves) thrown into jail for protesting violence and terror and torture. And one's reflectiveness grew as the crisis grew. One must not be fanatical, or afraid of being wrong. One must be afraid only of silence, silence in the face of a simple violation of humanity, of the right to life on the part of the innocent. One was forbidden to take his place thoughtlessly in the ranks of those who remained silent. He must also attend to the cries of those at a distance—perhaps he must be providential and point to a new stage of things: renewal from without. God does not act superficially; He grants us tragic prophets. And not always from the ranks of the believers.

The structure, the last to be converted. Or so we begin to believe when communication has been lost. Perhaps this is the true domain of the principalities—the loss of belief in our power to be converted by one another.

A methodology of history arises out of apprehended mystery, and not vice versa. To reverse the process is to justify what one is doing (or worse, what has won acceptance as a rule or method) into the mystery itself.

When we begin to think about the unthinkable we may even be ready to begin thinking about the resurrection.

To draw into one's self the order of the world is to draw into one's self the disorder of the world. But not in equal measure or by a like method. To draw on an order of things is an act of grace, a submission before reality; to draw on disorder is the price of living in the world. The purifying of order by the conquest of disorder cannot proceed outside one's own soul. It is the highest activity of the soul itself.

We would like to be able to say, I can judge the world without being judged. But we know it is impossible. Because disorder lies at our heart. The drama without is the drama within, at least in an exemplary way; the one is joined to the other by the undefeated possibility of evil—the human potential for self-destruction.

The tide of events, the facts of life, including malice and evil as well as goodness and light—this is evidence of the existence of God, as well as evidence for the fact of no God at all. It depends on who reads the text, and under what powers. In this sense, there is no evidence for or against, no evidence powerful enough to converge on the creation or the dissolution of mystery. There is only a choice of one by Another which, as admission and welcome, is the denial of the final validity of all evidence. Both believer and unbeliever stand at the closed door, the wall without a break. But One breaks in; we believe.

Until the evidence (which in itself is contradictory) is illumined from without, the atheists have much on their side. And insofar as believers think the "evidence adds up to" God they are wrong. They have emptied the mystery and filled it with themselves, or with their own apologetic—which is perilously close to atheism.

There is a mode of activity that advances further along a line of thought or action already begun by others, or that translates thought courageously from the printed pages into visible and conclusive action. And this is prophecy, though of a lower order.

And there is action that has no obvious link with what went immediately before. It has no immediate parentage in previous imagination. It appears suddenly, like springs in a desert where no one has prospected, and where men had often passed by— some to die of thirst; some to come on known oases. But the springs were there—in prehistory, in the subconscious, in the spiritual voices audible to only a few. Such activity walks the fine line between hallucination and revolt on the one hand, and the highest, indispensable, saving action on the other. How to judge it or place it? Only time will fully tell. But a judgment upon it is strongly helped if a sacrificial death has ended the work—the more shocking and undeserved, the better. All life is inundated by the blood which then falls, and gathers in a single visible gift. One must not live too long.

The saddest of sights: men who created their lives out of moral passion, ideals, imagination. Then, joining the establishment in their old age, they became gray eminences in the outer offices of bureaucrats, where the wind of hope and truth seldom penetrate. One can live too long.

For other men, grown old in a far different way, the establishment simply has never existed as anything real or attractive. So in their old age, life never takes the form of a shelter at the end of the night. The end of the night, that is, cannot be conceived of as a haven that men had built or stood guard over or decided entrance into. What such heroes looked for could only be conveyed by the mysterious term "heavenly dwellings." God alone was the architect of their eternity.

Simone Weil remained outside, for the love of "all the immense stretch of past centuries, all the countries of the Blacks, all the profane life of the white races." A decision taken in all serious-ness. But what of universality? She was not able to see evidence of it in what she saw of us. Which is to say, the Church did not open a door on all times and all places for her. But what shall we say for those within, who also want the strongest links with "the past centuries, the Blacks, and profane life"? Are we to be denied this?

The denial of this can be disciplinary; it can never be spiritual. Quite the opposite. Which saying does not attempt to answer the difficulty. It is not to be solved by recourse to an abstract liberty, which, because it is publicly unverified by the believer, is never entirely possessed. How do I know I am in spiritual contact with these others if, even in cases that are quite legitimate, I am not allowed to stand with them?

And why, in any case, should my passion for universality be less strong than that which burns in "unbelievers"?

In certain cases a thing is called for (necessary) simply because it is possible. If I have food and a hungry man stands at my door, charity must go out in his direction. The alternatives are narrowed, in a sense, by a moral order demanding fulfillment. In such a case, charity is the only possible fulfillment. A single action joins me to a universal order.

But no such parallel exists when a technological breakthrough seems to establish a necessity—that of taking the next step, what-ever its nature or implications. There is no justification in as-serting, nuclear arms are now possible, therefore they must be constructed. Or in asserting, the Bomb is constructed, therefore we can use it. In such judgments, charity is not only not operative; it is also positively excluded. And further steps, whatever auton-omy or magical omnipotence they assert, are essentially moral cutoffs. They have no part in the moral adventure of man. They are pretensions to *hubris,* and they call men aside to madness.

The General, standing grand as a Rembrandt burgher in his military stars and crowns, with his massive hand on a globe, is retiring. But he has also written a book on nuclear deterrents, which qualifies him as an architect of man's future. Among his qualifications to speak for us: He planned the first fire raids on Tokyo.

He planned the raids from afar, setting fires that destroyed some 100,000 innocent noncombatants. And he has lived un- troubled and feted into an honorable old age. We have gone beyond the Greeks; the Furies are dead, or silent.

Military chaplains who conduct services at posts of training and at the front lines. They brought the word of God into unlikely corners of the world. Most of them, in all their military careers, never were troubled in conscience about the commands, the tactics, the bombings, the tortures, the growing waves of savagery, the exterminations, the demand for unconditional sur- render. They returned to parishes at peace, with a sigh of relief no doubt, but with no questions. They had been part of a war machine, urged into uniform "by the needs of our boys." Now they are part of a peace machine, for as long as the peace can last. But how many of them will ever stand in judgment on the machine, in order to stand within Christianity? This can indeed be questioned. It is the only question. And it is never posed.

Indeed does Christianity awaken questions at all, in the sense that the universe always awakens man to a living interrogation point, and thence to wisdom? Or is the faith a kind of drugged seedcake tossed out to seduce Cerberus? We wish to pass through the ominous gates, but not at the price of death.

"People like myself want, not a world in which murder does not exist—we are not as crazy as that. What we want is a world in which murder is not legitimate" (Camus).

True, we were seeking an end to all wars—to war as such. If this is unrealistic and naive, consider that it is the purpose of all thinking men, and has been so for a thousand years, as men have sought to deal with human conflict. We are all utopians in spite of the brutal evidence of history which would seem to award the palm only to the Machiavellians or the armament kings. No; all good men are utopians; they struggle for peace in the teeth of conflict. But our stand assumed that no war could be waged in the hope to end war; and this was where our debate really began.

"But aren't you being used?"

Of course we are being used. We might even be used well, as we hope to be; or be used up. But what we are sure of is that we are not being manipulated. We are sure because practically every one of our confreres in the peace movement is also a friend. We have not suddenly taken our place next to strangers on some whim or enthusiasm of the moment. Our lives have converged on other lives—the way the deepest human convictions come together to nourish one another. An occurrence which others found almost impossible to imagine, because they had never experienced it: a fraternity of conscience.

The status of a minority responsibly saving the majority from its illusions of infallibility should be nothing new to a democracy. But to be a minority in wartime is no picnic. It means paying the price of not having one's mind imprisoned by the sloganeering of those who have "gone all out." Indeed, war stops all questions. And peace can only begin again when the questions natural to thinking man are again in the air.

We were not the neo-orthodox of anyone's order. If we could be open to the charge of simplicism, it was not ultimately due to our lack of political realism, or to our inept writing. It was because we insisted that Christ was a living God, that Christianity had something to say in moral crisis. Among most Christians the view was indefensible and even scandalous. If Christ had anything to say in a war atmosphere, surely His speech should be filtered down, "cleared" with the military. The word of God, applied here and now, should be subjected to censorship. Whereas we suggested that the opposite was true: All men, even men of power, stand under His judgment. The Church, not the Pentagon, is the keeper of man's soul.

Against an ideology one can only summon another ideology. And at this point any means becomes defensible. A purpose, even a pure one, is throttled by impure means. But suppose that against an ideology one were merely to appeal to men—to believing men, men who live in the mind, men who are responsible?

When one begins appealing to men, the means being used by either side are suddenly illumined—pure or impure, defensible or atrocious—whereas appeal to ideologies summons the worst to meet the worst. One system is defended, precisely by launching a bigger arsenal into a larger area. The innocent, the unprotected, the poor, must fend for themselves. Thus the first mark of the evil means constructed by rival ideologies is precisely this: The innocent are the first victims of "confrontation."

The redemptive openness of Buddha, and the suffering servanthood of Isaiah. Perhaps the forms of this universality of compassion today are: (1) recognition of one's own poverty—a matter of existence willed by God and aggravated by our pretension and childishness and egoism; (2) willingness to sacrifice and to share.

Changes that count are never mere biological developments, even by analogy. They are the fruit of that questioning mind that stands opposite the universe in a lover's quarrel—in love, but not mesmerized by love.

Rejoicing in deep joy where we stand, not in the stance of an iron post, but of a living tree. Or better— a people on the march, a darkness in which God may speak ("today, if you hear His voice"); a desert dawn or evening, with everything—tomorrow's fate, today's sustenance, the presence of others, nature, the transfigured silence—a mystery!

The world being what it is today, the assent of divine faith must often take the form of protest. I believe; therefore I dare disagree with the deep wrong implicit in a given situation. If we understood the faith, how true it would be that baptismal fonts would be antechambers not of churches but of prisons.

The reason no breakthrough occurs in ideas is that no breakthrough has occurred in men of thought. We wrong the mystery of truth when we conceive it as a simple process of inference and refinement. What is often called for is a conversion of intellectuals—a change of heart that will bring the truth into new and often shocking perspectives. Or that will allow a man to assent with his whole being to the truth he had accepted ideally, or inertly, or abstractly. Giving one's self to the truth has a tragic history. The history of ideas, on the other hand, is a sterile, effete hobby. It includes the ideas of tyrants, warmongers, and intellectual bigots. And it has brought only disaster to the world.

Thinking with the Church requires thinking with the world. The Church is indeed a center—but without a circumference it becomes a mere *ens rationis*—an invisible point.

"O God, plead my cause!" This is exactly what God has promised to do—indeed to be. A God who is not stranger or spectator or prosecutor. One who is not outside the "case"—the predicament of man—but who is precisely, Defender: "I will send you an Advocate."

A human life goes forward somewhat like a gathering wave toward its shore. The whole wave does not arrive together. At certain points, strength is dissipated and the crest dissolves; it may be in selfishness or in service. But how much of man is imperfect at the hour of his death. This is the mystery of his attractiveness. He is delivered to death, not as a superman but as a used and exhausted servant. And the beauty that marks Him in death is not that of an empty corpse, but the play and light of an absent spirit. He will be perfect, but elsewhere.

An astonishing sight: religious men for whom times of crisis present no occasion of anguish, no moral dilemma. They seem already dead—or perhaps unborn. But the analogy is too simple to explain a life which is almost completely nonproblematic. What spiritual force can indeed bring into birth a convinced and contented nineteenth-century mind? Or what resurrecting power can bring back to life one who has died without ever having lived in his own times?

PART TWO

Journey from
Sharpeville to Selma

V

ONE HAD the sense, rightly or no, of having landed here before. It was not merely the red ground underfoot, swirling in the hot wind, kicking up a red cloud around cattle and men and cars. Nor the earth coming to life again, after winter in July, or winter in January. Nor the plain that ran flat to the horizon in both places, far as the eye could reach; dogwood, magnolias, Spanish moss on the buttonwood and scrub pine. One had seen all this before; but one had seen something more, something that clung to the heart and almost defied the reach of words.

It was in the air. It held the eyes of people to a stranger's eye—too long or too briefly for comfort. It was in the air; it was in the shuffle of the Negroes, it clung to the unpaved streets, the open garbage, the children playing in the dirt. It could almost be touched; it was pervasive as memory; something terrifying and obscene. It lingered around the troopers, played and played back from faces too alike to be entirely human. It was death, and violence, and years of terror.

It was the memory of Sharpeville. More than eighty had died in a burst of vicious, pure, unpremeditated violence. It was in the air of Selma; the air bore it like a groan—the memories of some twenty years. Through these town roads, the body of a black man, roped like a venison to the sheriff's car, had been driven into the Negro area. Go slow—slow. Let them see who's in charge here. It was in the air. Fifteen years ago a black man, arrested "for talkin' back" on the word of a cranky white woman, had been murdered in Selma jail. "An unknown policeman" had entered his cell and shot him. His body was dumped off on his family. No verdict, no investigation. But the town has not forgotten.

It is still in the air. Jimmy Lee Jackson, shot in Marion for defending his mother against a trooper's club, died in Good Samaritan Hospital here. He had powder burns on the skin of his belly. The barrel had been pushed to its closest range, and fired twice. The Negroes remembered that night. When they tried to send hearses from Selma to Marion to pick up the

wounded, lying untended in the streets, their answer had come
from the sheriff's office: Come in here, you'll get what the rest
got; I'll dump you in the river.

Could the whites forget, in Selma, or in Johannesburg? In
Johannesburg they can, or almost. Once, Sharpeville had been
a bitter memory; in '61, the economy was on the verge of a
panic. Investors had taken their money elsewhere. There was
talk that blood and revolution would follow on the deaths of
the blacks. Small countries had begun a boycott; the British
Commonwealth had expelled South Africa. But the great powers,
and especially the United States, came to the rescue. In one
year, 1961, we contributed almost the entire amount needed
in foreign exchange to push the trend up once more; some 150
millions poured in to stop the crisis.

The slump was not only eased, it was entirely reversed. By
June of 1963, with continued U.S. help, South African gold and
foreign exchange reserves had more than tripled, to reach a
record high. The boom was on. And no one, not even the hard-
headed, cares to say where it will stop.

Time, they say, is a slow healer. Money, one thinks, works
faster. One American businessman calls South Africa "tantaliz-
ing" to investors. "We know the people and the government, and
we back our conviction with our reputation and our dollars."

But money has not come into beleaguered Selma. In the short
weeks since Negroes and northern whites declared nonviolent
war, business has dropped by fifty per cent. And time the healer
has not arrived yet. He is kept at bay; the false peace is inter-
dicted. The Negroes have seen to that; from Martin Luther King
to the farmhand who shows up to march on Tuesday with Monday's bandage still bloody on his head. Indeed, the trooper is
right when he cries, zooming like a tortured gadfly on his motor-
cycle from end to end of the marchers: "I've never seen anything
like this in all my —— life!"

Neither has the nation. Neither has the Church. Who ever
heard of a Church, North or South, that has rung, day after
day, week after week, with the unending songs, the prayers, the
sermons; a Church that spilled into the streets a people ready for
whatever hell the troopers are ready to bring down on them:
dogs, horses, whips, tear gas, billies? What liturgy prepares men

and women and children for Lingo and Clark and Connor? What faith arms men by forbidding them arms, tells them to march when they can, to kneel when they cannot, to face the oppressor —maybe even to convert him? The questions are fierce, and for the moment (for white Americans) unanswerable. But the point is clear; the questions are real questions, as real as the broken bones and the blood; as real as the new hope.

Monday, March 15. We came in, thirty-five strong, from New York, in time for the memorial service for Reverend Reeb. We were from Harlem and Manhattan and Brooklyn, Negroes and whites, layman and priests. Selma was quiet as a mill pond; but the quiet was ominous; the pin had been pulled, the depth charge dropped. Children wandered in the sun, the stores were open, the fresh tourist signs were out: WELCOME TO SELMA . . . SHANNON HOTEL. Then, we approached. Browns Chapel, the reality of Selma hit like a tight fist.

The church was ringed with Clark's troopers. They lounged in the open cars, feet hung out of doors and windows, eyes half closed in the sunlight; helmets, billy clubs, a stereotype of sleepy brutal power; the day of the iguana. Our car circled the church for blocks—no way in. Finally, we parked and walked through.

The church was packed. The TV cameras, the newsmen were there in force, tired out but still there. The nation needed to see this; better, since Sunday, it even wanted to see. A shabby backwater church, that had sheltered and comforted generations of Negroes, and had rung with the passion and anguish of a trodden people, was for this week the heart and focus of America. In it, the most astounding ironies were being taken for granted. Black store hands and field workers sat beside distinguished theologians. Hawaiians met New Yorkers, believers shook hands with the unchurched, beatniks sang along with nuns. Men who differed in every conceivable respect—faith and race and culture—found themselves bewildered by a sudden unity whose implications went far beyond the unpredictable days they were enduring together. But they knew beyond any doubt that they would never again be the same men who had lived Before Selma.

Light by light, individual purpose was fused in the incandescent arc of Negro courage and Negro passion. Free-e-e-dom. Free-e-e-dom. They sang it together, the skilled and the ignorant, the neophyte and the victim. Some of them knew what they sang. But the others were learning.

The speeches began. Walter Reuther, an Orthodox Bishop, a Catholic Bishop, two Ministers, and finally Martin Luther King. The words ranged from noble to bathetic, and back again. King's voice was ragged with exhaustion, the strain of vigils and of decisions, the killing round of the weeks, from courts to streets to meetings and back again, with the responsibility of sending the crowds out to face Jim Clark.

One thing was clear. This was the Negro's day. We were, at long last, at his side. But even the newsmen were not sure why we were there. They were not even convinced that we knew why; one of them asked us, in words that were not especially flattering: Why have the Catholics gotten into the act? We were not sure either, in a way that could easily be formulated. But it was something like an ethic of the guts; some things cannot be disposed of, in peace, by moral tics over headlines, even in 1965.

Almost everyone one could think of was there: men of concern, men of theology, nurses, teaching nuns, writers, rabbis, artists, students. Where's so and so? He was either there (one would meet him or see him in the crowd) or he was on his way or he had stopped and gone. And all week long, the vigils, the prayers, the Negro hospitality (our money was no good, anywhere), the cheerful faith, the contrast of ascetic purity and puritanism on the rampage, of birth pangs and the desperate lunges of moral death, the swift free calls to prayer and song and march, and the knowledge that slavery hemmed us in—what is the Church, anyway? Is it where we came from, or is it here, being created by Negroes and their white acolytes?

In any case, it was the black man's day, his week; one might say, his week of creation. He had been conceived and born at Bloody Bridge, at all the bloody crossroads of the nation, weeks and years before Selma. Could he, this week, bring us over that Bridge, to birth? He might; love is a marvelous midwife.

Johannesburg, the black township, Good Friday, 1946. The Gospel of Saint John was read in Zulu. And they crucified Him there; it was about the third hour. . . . The sea of color, the immobile, intent faces, men, women, children, hundreds strong, seated on the earthen floor. What could a white man say to them? what could a white priest say? He could say something surely; he might even say a new thing. He might say that Christ had died for all men, even for white men. He could take up his cross, hammered together by fate, propped up, waiting, visible to all. In South Africa, his cross was simply the fact of being a white man with some remnant of conscience. He could say in public, while the Special Branch Police lounged against the walls taking notes, that he was unworthy of his black brothers; that some day the white man might conceivably leave off being their executioner.

Monday, March 15, Selma. The long memorial service is almost over. Hardly any discomfort is evident; Negroes are used to standing, kneeling, waiting; and the whites are learning. The weather outside is Alabama spring time, a frayed and dusty glory. Dogwood and magnolia are coming to flower. The benediction has been pronounced over the memory of Reeb. Flowers bank the speakers' stand. Someone has pinned to the front of the pulpit a drawing from a northern newspaper; it shows a wreath of thorns fastened to a gravestone, the tomb of James Reeb. Martin King has spoken. And then, the announcement comes; the march is permitted by court order. Three by three, in silence, we are allowed by the courts of Alabama to march on the court-house of Selma. It is to be a memorial march for James Jackson and James Reeb. Prayers at the courthouse are permitted; we can even sing.

Whites and Negroes, after all the bitter years, after black heroism and white anger, after Birmingham and Marion and St. Augustine—after all this, both sides are fused together by one fact, a bitter event which neither side wanted but which each side knew in its heart must come to pass. Each side now had a martyr.

For the Negroes, the irony is very nearly complete. They have had to wait and wait for the whites—when will they stand with us, or march with us? And the whites have waited for a death, before they could be moved. For the Negroes, martyrdom was nothing new at all; it was old as their American history. It had begun with lynchings and disappearances and bodies pulled from rivers. Most of the Negro martyrs were nameless. But one of them, otherwise obscure and humble, had died in Selma; and Selma, by a convergence of happenings beyond all prediction, had exploded.

The explosion was triggered by a white man's death. The blow had been launched by whites; they had struck down a minister of the Gospel. It was a wound with a difference; it lay on the body of the white community.

Time indeed might heal it. Give us time . . . you can't push this thing too fast. . . . But no time was allowed. The Negroes granted time no place. They had been clocked too long by whites; Clark and Lingo had had too much time; time for troopers, time for gas, time for Bloody Bridge. The end was there in sight. We started out.

The Gospel of Saint John, in the Zulu tongue, so strange to American ears; sibilants and the clicking of tongues, with only the names Jesus, Mary, Peter, John, coming through. And about the third hour, they crucified Him. . . . A white priest, in the pulpit of the black church; my fellow Christians. He can hardly remember what he had to say to them. But at the end, the veneration of the Cross. A great wave starts forward: mothers with children, young men, the very old. Three priests move among them, holding the crucifix to their lips. And spontaneously, as is the way with Africans, the chant starts; first, as one voice, hardly rising above the sough of bare feet, that sound which above all sounds is like the sea, on a mild evening. The song is the Zulu dirge for a fallen warrior. They are bearing Him homeward to his village after battle. His name is Jesus, great King, black Warrior. Easily, with infinite delicacy and natural-ness, the song breaks into harmony; two parts, then four, then eight, as a yolk divides, or a cell . . . Jesus, great Warrior, we mourn you. O the beauty, the youth, the empty place. Who shall plead for us, who shall lift our faces, who shall speak wisdom?

The Zulus have a saying: he who is behind must run faster than he who is in front. Even to the Cross. Even when the Cross is held in white hands. Shall the white man time us, even to the Cross? Does he any longer even know the way?

The strangest thing about the march to Selma courthouse was the utter silence in town. That, and the faces of the troopers.

There was a trooper for every marcher, someone said. Almost, but not quite. The three hundred who left the Church were joined, like streams to a great river, by those who had arrived outside, and were waiting; some two thousand in all. The town had gone silent, as though a great hand were clapped to its mouth, at five o'clock on a workday evening. Traffic was lined up at corners, storekeepers in their doorways; the troopers' cameras were clicking in the faces of the clergy. (Good to know we'll be in Jim Clark's scrapbook!) But mostly silence. Except that, all along the route, the transistors kept telling us and the nation what it was like, what it could never be like again, in Selma on a spring evening.

The breakthrough had come, irresistible as spring. You could see it, whoever you were, trooper or housewife, white or black. You could hate it like the approach of death, or feel it in your bones like the nudge of Christ on Lazarus—but it was there, for all the world to see. In the dusk around Courthouse Square (that's Jim Clark's courthouse—but no more, no more) the big TV lights went on in a wink, punctual as dawn, the lights no Negro had dared hope to see. The prayers began; for the dead, for the living, for the persecutors. Martin King laid at the glass doorway a purple wreath: "For James Reeb," the crepe said. But at that moment, the worried, porcine face of Jim Clark was peering through the glass. Jim Clark, framed in a burial wreath; beyond the mild ghost of James Reeb, the death of southern power and conscienceless law. For the Negroes, it was a moment delicious beyond words; requiescat Jacobus.

In the African reserve, it was autumn; but the autumn had come on so gently it might have been an Alabama spring. Passion flowers and magnolias and wild roses, the last of them. But under the dusty clouds that followed cars and men like their shadows, hardly a flower or a blade of grass. We were in the last of the old city reserves, marked by the city for bulldozing. The serpentine alleys, the crazy shacks, were to come down. One thought, It wouldn't take much of a push to bring all this to the ground.

Coming up: a government plan, complete to the last nail and brick. New dormitories for the black city workers, male and female dwellings side by side, housing for some sixty thousand. (But as usual, when the Verwoerd government plans for the

Africans, there's a hidden card. The workers are in fact country people, up from the impoverished reserves to seek jobs. Some sixty per cent of the men are married, by conservative estimate; the government understandably supplies no figures. Many have young families started. They leave wives and children behind, and the pass laws lock them in the city. The government is in fact promoting and legalizing the breakup of African families and easing the blow by providing easily available prostitution.)

In the reserve in Johannesburg, everything is inside the fences: the schools, the stores, the church and rectory and convent. They were all to come down. The families would be moved some twenty miles out, into paved streets and brick homes. (The finest in Africa, the government declares. Where else in our continent does each black family have its own home, constructed by the state, with a yard and space for a tree or two? A family can even buy its own home on credit. . . . But a family can never own the land on which the home stands.)

We toured the reserve. Hopelessness, torpor, the crime rate soaring. But the priests are welcome. They are the only whites who can move in and out with a measure of safety or the hope of a greeting, in all this jungle. We returned to the rectory. Out of the darkness of the yard, a man and child emerged. They had waited there for an hour "to see the priest who spoke this afternoon. Everyone is saying, He spoke for us, he said something for us. I wanted to thank him; I brought my small daughter to meet him."

Selma, Tuesday afternoon, March 16. Jim Clark's troopers have raced into Montgomery. A march was undertaken there, and violence has erupted. We in Selma will march also, in sympathy and protest. The wounded are lying in the street of the capital, after a mounted charge. There is a call for doctors and nurses; two nuns get up and leave the church.

Jim Clark has had another frustrating day. Without troopers, he had to keep some hundreds of marchers off the streets, with only his posses and a few men in Conservation Department cars. Baker is not in evidence; he seems to know that Clark cannot do much harm without his bullies. But Clark races up and down Sylvan Street, in front of Browns Chapel, his white Chrysler careening like a dreadnought under fire, stopping the line at one end, then at the other. He swings around to a halt, races from the car ("Man, he'll end up dead; he's too fat for all that runnin' "), confronts the line at the north end; on signal the marchers turn south. Back to the car on the run, down to the other end. But the marchers turn once more, facing center. The line breaks at the middle; those in the center turn at right angles, into the housing project yards. Too narrow for the Chrysler; Clark has to take the long way round. And by then, some are almost to the courthouse. Frantic, sweating, he turns them back.

Into the church again. We pray briefly, a Southern Conference minister leading; We ask You that the black belt may become a belt of light. . . . We stand where the law has been misused, where the innocent have been struck down. . . . Be with us and our leaders. . . .

A young Negro in overalls speaks to us. "Clark's not going to tell us we can march one day and not march the next. We're going to keep moving. They're bludgeoning people in Montgomery this afternoon, charging them with horses. We're going to reach our courthouse and pray there." Another Negro approaches the speaker and whispers the news. Clark has the Church ringed with police; he's gotten them back into town. "Now this is the worst thing of all. He's trying to keep us in here, against all law. So we're goin' out. We want the priests and ministers to lead; if we're to be beaten, they ought to take it first. Will you go?"

We will. We strike up a song, and start. This might be it.

It was worse, and better, than one had imagined. It may have been all the clerics, the white faces among the black. But there was no charge of the helmeted ring; they stood there, they didn't give an inch; but they didn't move in either. And in Selma, after the past week, that was something new.

In front, the white priest, the rabbi, and the Negro minister confronted Clark. The newsmen moved close, the TV took it all in; five minutes of passionate exchange, then the decision. A cleric in front turned to the line, spoke quietly, and knelt. Men and women and children went down on knee, as though under the pressure of some sudden wind. The TV commentator said it into his mike, stepping among the crouching figures to get his pictures. But we already knew it: "It looks like another long night in Selma."

PART THREE

To Limbo and Back:
A Latin American Journey

VI

CUERNAVACA

THE IMPORTANT thing was not that injustice had happened *to me*. The important thing was that injustice had occurred at all; that injustice was still possible—an evil of this kind, the defeat of good work, the silencing of truth. This bit deep. But the purification of evil was the most important thing of all; first of all in myself—neither bitterness nor vengeful thoughts, nor even malingering around the idea of personal vindication. The desire for purification must advance into the possibility of creating purity in others, and especially in systems of authority which had become the persecutor, and in that measure were impure.

To turn others toward peace: One does not walk out of that vocation in walking across a border. Not even when one is forced across. For one cannot be forced out of his own peace, nor out of the making of peace. One can only be forced by the hand of God into another ambiance, another opportunity. In this sense, one is forced into the realization of what is always struggling to be born in the Church, of what cannot be brought to birth without a struggle. The intelligence of Christ so often took up this theme; in death, in new birth, in new age of man, in new quality of life.

Unity is always cheap in the beginning. One is born into it; one inherits it. Such unity is a grace, a foothold. The falsity comes when one lives off his inheritance without trading in it, without giving it away, or starting anew. In such a case, the bloodline becomes a curse, the inheritance a slavery.

To the degree that life becomes conscious, it becomes charged with responsibilities. And becomes universalized. And yet more and more concrete. *Pax in parvis et in multis.* And conversely. The irresponsibility and regression implied in "leaving history to form itself"—or in leaving history to others, or assailing it with the stereotypes of one's own betrayals of truth.

77

We seek a morality which builds itself from a convergence of values—lives press in on us and we are powerless to remain unconscious of them. They pour out on us their cries of lives betrayed, sold, neglected. To construct a conscience from such lives, from the living.

A time of war judges the time of peace that has gone before, and the quality of those who built the peace. Were they truly peaceful men, or were they sunning themselves along a wall they had not helped to raise? To go along with such a peace is very like going along with war.

The price of a false peace is as high as the price of a hot war. In fact, the cost of the first amounts to exactly the inevitability of the second.

A time of division, of misunderstanding, and of friction, may well seem the least auspicious time of healing or of reconciliation. And yet, when love is in question, the opposite may also be true. The worst of times may be the best of times.

One who has been evicted from his normal community may well be "the least of these"—the least qualified to speak of peace and unity. And yet the opposite may be true: A testing of spirits may reveal that the worst of men has something in his favor, something to offer others.

A time of war may be the least favorable time in which to speak for peace. Much is against it; frenzy, conflicting loyalties, and newly inflamed fears drive men's passions forward with a boiling intensity. Who will have the energy and staying power to confront the times, even to create a countercurrent, a kind of temperate Gulf Stream, choosing its own mysterious direction, maintaining its own temperature?

One must accept the ironies of life and take up the tasks of life. Disgraced or not, foolish or wise, living in ill times or good, we are what we are, we are where we are. The actual world is our only world. We must go forward; we must accept all that men say of us, however painful or unfair it be. The times allow for no delay. Life grants us no space for idleness, regrets, the pursuit of illusions. The work of peace must go on, in hardiness and steadfast good humor. We must consent to being ourselves, to being the unworthy vessels of God's word, to working with others, to the slow inching forward of compassion and hope.

What is the task before us? It is as large as life itself, and remains so even when times of crisis or war narrow it to the compass of a needle's eye, to a simple *no* to war and violence. If we must pass through the needle's eye, must take an unfrequented road, still our journey must not be solitary or capricious. It must be a journey with men and for men. It must form the largest possible company which is commensurate with a good conscience. It must include men who agree with us wholly, men who disagree in part, men who confront us with unwelcome alternatives. All are our brothers; it is their task as well as our own. We journey toward man. We all hear the same cry in the darkness —the wounded and the violated, the neglected poor, the victims of our history, those in whose destruction we have had part.

A time of exile may be the worst of times to assert one's solidarity with others, with his nation, his church, his brothers across the world. Let there be no romanticizing about the enchantment lent by distance. Exile is a terrible burden, a terrible weight. Even when understanding and welcome and new tasks are offered to such a one, the fact remains that his life has been terribly dislocated; he is thrust into a life for which he is grossly unprepared. He must abandon those who had depended on him, rightly or excessively. He must put aside his efforts to construct something rational and ongoing, a vision of life which drew on local community and circumstance, a vision of peace to which war itself was ironically contributing. But sometimes all this is disrupted. One will have some day to pick up the pieces; indeed, he has no real assurance that he can ever do so with those persons whose thought and example were part of the passionate fabric of his heart.

This is the hardest thing of all: to accept an impasse, a problematic, the dead end which life as one has known his life has in fact reached. In such a situation, which is my actual one, there can be no solution, in the proper sense of the word. Life, with the values and opportunities and joys one had known, has ground to a halt. Life has become crisis, and the crisis is insoluble, humanly speaking. Or at least let me say, Whatever resources or ingenuity I can summon offer me no present way out.

Or rather, only one way leads out. It offers not a solution at all, or a logical outcome. It offers no more than today offered, no more light, no more understanding, no healing. Almost no hope at all—at least not in the ordinary sense of the word.

What form, then, will life take, since it must take some form, supposing that one is to go on living? I can only say: The shape of my life, broken by human hands, must be formed again by other hands. I can see no other way; the problematic must yield to the mystery.

The mystery of the Cross. It is the mystery of this war, which has destroyed so many lives, including the moral lives of those who destroy. A war that has now reached perilously into my own life and destroyed its former shape, deflected its energies, disrupted its friendships, made of my life an occasion of division instead of the sign of unity I had hoped for.

An acceptance of the presence of mystery implies a lucid understanding of one's self and of others. One cannot claim to master life so long as he is ignorant of life. The obsessive longing for peace at any price, the willingness to barter valuable men for the cheap grace of good order, the dread of responsibilities implicit in friendship—all these are germane to the mystery I speak of. They are the ingredients of the cup of life itself—not, indeed, the only ingredients, since life is a rich vintage and offers but love and joy and heroism as well as other things. But we must speak of *this* cup, the taste of its contents presently on our lips. And the taste is that of gall, so extremely, so purely and outrageously bitter that one can perhaps conclude that no human ingenuity could have devised its essence. It is a vintage of God—or of Satan. Or, absurdly, of both.

So there is a problem of evil, and there is a mystery of evil.

The first is a product of history, explainable to history, assuaged to a degree, within history. Its nature is not of formal interest to me. Or let me at least say: Such evil could not create me as a man any more than it could destroy me as a man. It can awaken energies or render them lax and lazy. Its omnipresence can arouse compassion or despair. It can send my hand to my pocket or send me on a conventional religious mission. It can command gestures without content. But its power over me goes only so far, only so far into my eyes or skin or soul as to leave them intact, neither greatly offended nor painfully awakened. I remain what I am though a beggar is before me, though an accident occurs down the street. I sit in the sunlight; I continue with my dinner. My moral life takes its food and drink, hears and sees and breathes the air of the world, evacuates its poisons. I remain a good intellectual animal, an approved domesticated specimen, a moral neutral. I deal inoffensively with the world; it offers me no reason for acting as anything but its colorless civil servant.

But the mystery of evil! Not a problem raised to the Nth degree. Nor a tag put arbitrarily on life simply because life has suddenly grown too big for my resources. A problem does not differ from a mystery because the problem has no evident answer, or is pure enigma.

The gesture proper to a problem before one is the taking up of a plumbline or calipers. Proper means are chosen and put resourcefully to work. But the gesture proper to mystery cannot be termed a hopeless lifting and falling of one's hands! Indeed, if the workings of our spirit were visible we would see a response to mystery as something parallel to the summoning of man's body before an obstacle. *Fides quaerens intellectum.* Man wants to *know,* whatever the case. In the first, that of the problematic, he wishes to apprehend, to take the world to himself. In the second, he wishes to submit before a world which he confesses is larger than his resources. Problems are made for man in order—through their largeness and scope and puzzle once confronted—to make him more fully himself. Through solutions he enters into wider, and richer, implications of his universe. So, more surely, he enters into himself by way of the real world;

into his own body which is a world body; into a future which
he is able to bring nearer to himself, to declare as his own, and
so to make over into a true present.

But mystery? A will exists, which declares itself in a Man like
us, to be a Will of love, of concern. This Will has its design
in the world, is immanent in the world. But it is not subsumed,
not seized on by the world. Indeed, this Will brings the world
to a term that no confluence of history, no concentration of
energy or genius or human love could imagine—much less bring
about.

So the end of the problem is, at least in degree, an "arrival":
A man is in outer space; a disease is controlled; a theory is
vindicated. But before mystery, we stand perpetually before an
invitation so merciful, in fact, that our submission before it as
well as our powerlessness to possess it, is our greatest dignity.
To stand under that waterfall whose music is the promise, "More,
I will give more!"

It is a cliché that history is always renewing with surprising
events, that the truth is a matter to be lived, to be made present
in persons and communities. One way of doing this—one among
many—is to speak the truth. Which is not always possible, or
even expedient. Or even, let it be added, valuable. One recalls
the intemperate, insistent, all-disclosing kind of truth that leaves
men unmoved, leaves them only more stubbornly where they
were.

But to *live* the truth! Another matter entirely. So different
a matter, in fact, of so different an order, that it raises questions
of truth to another plane, sheds upon them an altogether unexpected radiance, grants them a new parabola of experience upon
which to draw. To be concrete: Is it better, in defense of the
truth, to be a man in community in New York exploring with
others the questions that animate us, drawing on the resources
concentrated there to protest evil, to uncover the alternatives of
man's life? Or is it better to be thrown back upon one's self
abroad, leaving his past like a diminishing wake, a memory that
is freshened only by occasional flutters? It is hard to answer.
Perhaps it is useless to attempt to answer. For if either activity

is valid as a human contribution, it must be true that in both
the range of life is in fact being extended, and that one is living
the truth for others. One is not wasting or violating life in
either circumstance; nor is he turning selfishly or surreptitiously
to his own ends.

The call to live the truth, rising from the pages of the Gospel
as well as from one's own being, thus can act in two comple-
mentary ways. It can chasten and subordinate one's activity to
the good of others, and it can act in order to interpret mis-
fortune. The first is the task of conscience as reproof and limiting
power of spirit upon egoism. The second is conscience as con-
soler. In both cases, we are speaking of the activity of the spirit
of truth.

"It is sad not to see any good in goodness" (Gogol). It is at
least equally sad not to see any evil in evil. In both cases we
are speaking of a consciousness that is fearfully alienated from
its proper world function. That function is the making of history,
which "walks upon two legs" or falls flat. But which must go
forward with man.

Perhaps from a historical point of view, this is what we are
living through in the Church, a spasm away from love back to
the iron breast of law, which is at once mother and destroyer.
As mother, offering a haven against the pain and threat of experience—two arms which purport to be the arms of God. But
in reality, a destroyer; the dark prison of the womb, the return
to which is a mortal danger to man. A historic misreading of
the text of history as God has actually communicated it: "I am
not in your iron idols—I am in mankind."

The response of churches during wartime is instructive. It
usually parallels the mentality of a nation at war. As such, it
represents a betrayal of the God of history—a falling back upon
a profoundly stereotyped, acquisitive morality—unassailable by
reason, unassailable also by the alternatives that actual life is
always offering to the living. Once such a "morality" is in command, and is presumed to be in possession, beyond criticism or

assault, literally anything is possible against "the enemy." And
the first victims of such action will, in the nature of things, be
the community of violence itself—it will be destroyed more
thoroughly than its enemies, or even its prophets. Man cannot
exist in a form of life that takes violence for its first method.
For such violence is waged against itself. The first fact of its
obituary is not that it has reduced the world to ashes—it is that
the giant perished by suicide.

Man is redeemed by Christ from the power of the law, from
abstract ideals, from merely human goodness, from laissez-faire
morality, from illusions of omnipotence, from reliance on tech-
nique as a way of controlling human lives, from pseudospiritual
jots and tittles, from the evil power of creating propaganda and
the evil slavery of submitting to it, from Hitler and Stalin, from
statism and racism, from communism and capitalism, from cold
and hot wars. Thus far and further: the liberation offered by
Christ. And further—even as far as history reaches, as far as its
unborn contaminations can reach. But the question remains:
How many men, how many Christians, desire this kind of freedom? It remains, as far as history has taken us, a gift suspended
in midair, a fruit never plucked. Or by only a few.

For the sake of abstract ideals, one can always become the
executioner of the living. This is the history of man b.c.—and
very nearly the history since. The *trahison des clercs*—the revolution crushed by "good men."

When the Church yields before the ideology of the state,
classifying men as enemies and remaining silent before methods
of wholesale slaughter, she in fact moves perilously near to
disbelief. She no longer proclaims her faith in the God Who
converts hearts to His justice. Equally she ceases to believe in
herself as Church. For to be Church is to be sinner, subject to
God's forgiving and renewing love. But to consent to war, to
cease to speak for the innocent, is to connive in such monstrous
guilt as places the Church herself beyond God's forgiveness. So
in the Viet Nam war, no official voice of the American Church
has yet condemned the indiscriminate bombing of the innocent,

the torture of prisoners, the burning of crops, or the suspension of civil liberties.

To oppose our present war on such grounds is justifiable, and, as we believe, expedient. But it is by no means the whole ground open to discussion. Even if not one civilian were killed, not one person reduced to beggary, not one person maltreated, and if somehow the fabric of social life remained intact through the years of war—and all these hypotheses lead us further into the absurdity of a claim that modern war can be just—many grave questions would remain. And the gravest revolves around this war as a paradigm of history. Does social change take place in these ways, under such leadership, by such methods, vitalized by such ideology? Is this our way into the future, for Asia and for ourselves? Or is the war not rather an historic abortivus, something whose birth may perhaps have been proper to nineteenth-century colonial history, but whose horror has been transplanted and forced into birth in the twentieth century?

Man is forbidden to kill. But a man steps into a uniform, is handed weapons, and commanded to kill. We have here a kind of walking into Alice's mirror, the ugly change that takes—that overtakes—man once he assumes his history. But *is* man required to be in history in such a way? For an eventual good, for moral or cultural reasons, can he be required or even allowed to kill? Does he express his solidarity with life, with the defense of life, by dealing out death? A most painful question. And one to which the past can give only the most unsatisfactory of answers. For the fact remains that once we have granted everything possible to the wars of history, once we have called them beneficial or inevitable or conducive of greater good than evil—after all this, we must still insist that the argument has little or no bearing upon present facts, for our past, as a history of war, presents really no alternatives to us.

We simply do not know what peace could have done, or peaceable arrangements, or the ingenuity of men who would have chosen peaceable change instead of violence. In the large print of history, we know only what violence accomplished. And even a history of violence is not so totally evil as here and there not to bring about some human benefit. But the question remains: What would methods of peace and compassion have wrought in circumstances where only war was wrought? What if the implications of the Sermon on the Mount had been realized, at a given period? Do we really know what might have been the alternatives to the Versailles Treaty if the Christian message of peace had been heard at the time of that treaty? Would the alternatives to unconditional surrender perhaps have saved Germany from her fatal response to Hitler, made it unnecessary to crush all other hope by demands of unconditional surrender, the dismemberment of her industry, and the impoverishment and humiliation of her people?

Thus, when we presume to judge our history something is always left out. The history itself is mutilated. We can measure our progress toward humanism or Christian life only by what data we have—which is to say, by the fury or comparative mercifulness of our wars. And this, by and large, is the history of the Church, in an analogous sense. In the world, fluctuations of violence; in the Church, long periods of consecrated violence. The other alternative, which we might call a concrete and living faith in Christ, is almost totally absent. Its social effects therefore lie beyond analysis; they have never germinated.

The history of war makes large claims for itself. Berdyaev, for example, repeats the claims with no particular attempt at analysis, and has little sense of what he is implying: "War has been the source of the lofty virtues of courage, honor, loyalty, chivalry, and nobility." This is an obvious recalling of the mythology of the Middle Ages. But what of these virtues, as the vision of the New Testament might have elevated them to a pure scheme of life? And what of the uncounted thousands whose destruction was the price paid for the exercise of such virtues?

It is not so much the presence of a world of sin that renders Christ inadequate or utopian in history. It is the presence of sin, concretely and historically, in Christians themselves. The defenders of the necessity of war, drawing on the history of war, inevitably regard the Sermon on the Mount from this point of view; if war is a historical necessity, it must follow that a kingdom of peace is purely eschatological. Which is to say, not merely that such ideology is in fact unrealizable, but more—that its existence depends radically on a further intervention of God, a day which no human resources can prepare for or bring to pass. But such reasoning is a highly specious use of the Gospel. The truth is that no history, however massively moving in one or another direction, can nullify the act of God, already brought to pass in Christ Jesus. The Kingdom is announced in the presence of God's son; a visible, active, audible reality, a body of believers, a kingdom of peace, of justice, and of love. Granted that such a group has not succeeded in converting the world to the ways of peace. But neither can the world declare, nor can a worldly church declare, that the peaceful work of the Kingdom is null and void, that every decision to submit to violence rather than to exercise violence, has not been a guarantee of the Lord's continued presence in time—an intervention of such constancy and power that, against it, violence could never quite possess the earth, never entirely claim man.

Insofar as the regime of the law is vigorously outside the regime of grace, attempts to return to the law and its methods amount to a rejection of Christ. The *sensus ecclesiae* is important and normative here. Men know when the church is working violence on them. They know because once more it is being preached that "man is made for the Sabbath," that the Church has come "to be served, not to serve," that "the outside of the cup and the plate" are to be kept clean for public view. And men know this more acutely when one among them, or many, lie untended in the ditch.

When faith in God is alive, there are no alternatives to man; neither state, nor ideology, nor cultural idolatries—nor, indeed, Church. There is, after Christ, only man. We Christians can have no quarrel with that. Or if we have a quarrel, our objections have the absurdity and invalidity of reproaches against God Himself.

When one begins to wonder what has happened to the former "signs and wonders" that marked the beginnings of the Church, he can conclude that God has withdrawn from man, which is really an accusation that God has reneged on his own promise. Or he can conclude that God has drawn closer to man, has sealed his promise afresh. I had rather opt for the latter. The great contemporary signs of God are the lives of men who speak up, and who die if necessary, for men. If this is an overhumanized version of things, it is the Incarnation which must stand trial for it. But religious faith, too, is on trial before the world, and the accusing judge is not on Sinai; he stands in the eyes of the undefended and violated, "the miner whom he shot down, the slave in the camps, the legions of persecuted throughout the world"—the litany of suffering that Camus knew so well. There can be no more armchair artists while men are being broken on the wheel of life. And no armchair Christians either.

The truest joy of a Christian is to know that his life serves; to know even obscurely that something is building up within him; to sense that an obscure fidelity, moment by moment, act by act, has brought him to where he stands at present. In apparently haphazard or brutal circumstances, he can witness in his life some larger creation than his life had prepared for; a mysterious beginning of a race which is at length fit for the world—fit for here and now, and for eternity. Something larger than himself! And exhilaration in all that is—in the midst of all that is apparently defeated and broken. An exhilaration, a gift to others, a life that shows when all is weighed in the balance, something left over, something available for others.

Suppose we were to disappear from the human landscape, in the sense that no merely inherited signs of our life on earth existed. To give up a history which is in so many aspects false, in what it is pretending to say, or persuading itself that it is saying. We must admit that a rather large percentage of what we are doing could disappear without any real damage to men. But force the same question further: What if the "Christian message" itself were silent for one generation? When the question is put in such a way, we perhaps come to the real point—which is that Christ might then have a chance to be heard, without the corruption of false signs offered by those who are irresponsible inheritors of the pure Word.

The intelligence that knows its frontiers. But how far beyond the frontiers it will be necessary to go, into no-man's land, or hostile territory, or paradise, or hell itself, in order to understand the difference between, first, frontiers which are the natural cutting edge of the mind itself; not so much the falling-off place of usefulness, but the meaning of the tool itself; and, secondly, the stinging inhibitions that cowardice or fear throw up against reality.

This frontier image seems to yield in favor of another: the mind as a kind of conscious heart, feeding on the actual impure world in order to invigorate it with conscious compassion, and to confer on it its own vocation—a passion for man.

Methods of dealing with the world: For some, books and the past; Don Juan or the saints, or a Christ made safe from the world and time. For others, a full effort to understand and submit to and deal with life. For the second, the past is a good paradigm, but it can be only a beginning. A necessary beginning which has purified the flesh and bones of the dead, winnowing them, releasing on the air their residue of spirit, all that in fact remains of men. No base power, no fingers closed on the throats of victims, no chant of conquest or despair. Of impurity, nothing. When one has breathed this essence, he is ready for the task of the living—which is, to begin an adventure that only life itself can seize on. He has also perhaps begun to vanquish death.

The Gospel message begins with a summons: "Go, be converted, serve." What follows is predictable. Men come timidly out of the murkiness and fear and slavery of their existence, to ask a question which the Gospel both answers and refuses to answer, the question that contains its own answer and yet hovers interminably on the air with grace and enchantment and gentleness: "Who is the Christ?" The question mobilizes life in the direction of a person. And He, once discovered, can never be claimed. He is only a new form of responsibility.

To inquire whether a life lived without an appeal to power could produce something for man—either in its silences or in its speech, a kind of art. Why not? At least, one sensed that exile was a good laboratory.

There are times in history when a tradition is large enough to nourish unusual men. There are times in the history of the Church when the truth sheds radiance on the world as it is. Christianity, at least for a time, has actually held the real world in hand, has spoken of it, and given it back something—a taste and smell of the living in the air, like the heavy scent from an autumn fruit tree, an exuberance, rot on the ground, groaning boughs at term.

One of the aspects of priestly anguish today is the absence of myths. So the priesthood must create its symbols out of itself, its attitudes, its rejections and follies, its weaknesses, even its sins; a kind of Pauline experience brought up to date. Bernanos did this. But the fact was, his scope was too small and too victimized by smallness. It was a village drama, and to that degree, admitting the nobility of his tragic hero, it was uninteresting. Men had not yet grappled with their world—a double ignorance was almost totally inhibiting—ignorance of the world and of the sacred. The sequence here is of the essence. A priestly life in the large cities, which is the real question today, is brutally assailed by the twin devils of intellectualism, and a disappearance into triviality. But there is very little *partage du midi*.

Nothing that excludes can exist for long. Except by feeding on itself. And in such a case it will shortly find itself indigestible and give up even that sorry exercise.

This may be the special gift of exile—to be excluded without excluding; indeed, to depart willingly, because the deepest meaning of banishment is that one has entered anew, into relationships with persons, by way of hope. And by way of building hope.

It is a terrifying thing to shoulder the hope of others, especially when they have ceased to hope for themselves at all.

Hopelessness in authority forbids others a future it could not first conceive for itself.

Why conceive of hope as a burden at all? It is in fact a kind of weightlessness proper to spirit; it has conquered the gravitational slavery of time and wrong, and already inhabits the future, a counterpoise to the world's burden.

To have no quarrel with the world is to become an object among things. Entirely reconciled, as a corpse is. But to have no friendship with the world?

To haul in nothing but certainties; to haul in only dead fish.

This self-justifying man: His life is marked by a spasmodic tic of instinctual life; his certainties are firmly buried in the past, and emerge only far enough to mark the edges of his father's landholdings. Many stumble over the marker, and curse it. In any case, the stick will never turn miraculously to green, or bear fruit.

The minor prophet; his life is understandable only by its distance from purity. A grace never offered, a moment dreaded, and adherence never cut away from his heart. He acts, but seeks justification for acting. He has not come to wholeness; which is to say, to absurdity. Men still find him explainable. He has too many defenders; he does not stand in his own light. He does not live in the darkness that only death can dissipate. Life is too clear to him, and death too dreadful: exactly a reversal of the order of reality.

For one who chooses to be free today, the choices are strait and biblical. One can be an exile, a prisoner, a condemned man, a Negro, a villager under the napalm. A choice is offered. And it is the faces which reveal that the choices have been authentic. In prison, at the point of death, in courtrooms—the faces of men. Tranquil, bold, finely sculptured by adversity, supple, without extravagance, without waste or superfluity. Men who have passed time and again from life into death, and miraculously back again. Witnesses of what an older tradition would call resurrection; which we translate, more modestly, men of hope.

Somewhere between the hopeless herd and the men of hope—
the Church. Neither one nor the other. But partaking of both.
And since the men of hope are never entirely defeated, there
remains enough hope to go on.

When the Church is incapable of reading the signs of the times,
she herself is obscured as a sign.

A world which lives in utmost poverty can allow for no
luxuries. And the most wasteful and enervating of all luxuries
is that of self-pity.

The example of Jesus is so pure, as well as so purifying, that
one hesitates to claim Him as one's own advocate in adverse
times. Tread softly; something dangerous is implied here. Swim-
ming in the murky waters of life, can one suddenly claim to be
a disciple simply because certain aspects of his life have been
challenged? Almost certainly not. There is a way of "claiming"
Christ for one's own which is profoundly alienating—both from
the real Christ, and from men. It is the height of illusion. It
is also an effective excuse for leading a half-conscious life. One
sees this at work socially in the Church at times, when the
Church claims Christ as its persecuted Body, ignoring the solidarity in sin which joins us, if the truth were told, to the
persecutor himself, both in history and in the present.

To be in history is to be a sinner. To be in sacred history is
to be hopeful.

"The people of God"—a dubious and preemptive title, given
the facts of life. We had best wait for God to confer some title
on us—in His own time, by a baptism of fire which life itself
pours upon us. The word of the prophets is something other
—"You have hoped for great things; hope for nothing." But this
is the birth of true hope.

The quest for clarity is almost always a folly until the facts
are in. And even when the facts *are* in, the search may be a form

of evasion so long as the truth remains unacceptable to consciousness. What are the facts of history, as living men assemble
them before us? They are not particularly palatable. Let us hear
from the Jews. Let us even hear from those of our own community who have suffered atrociously from the Church. Something of our need of divine mercy may emerge.

The only "pure" situation from which to speak is that of
suffering that has been undergone in at least a relative innocence.
But suffering men are strangely enough the last men of all to
speak, the most tentative. "At the edges, it is best to keep silence"
(Bonhoeffer).

VII

CARACAS
MANY are becoming aware of the need of conversation as a law
of the mind itself. But not many have yet looked deeply enough
into the mind, which must not only be fed by others but must
also be discriminating—in view of the laws that govern its activity, and of the food it takes. Not everything is health-giving;
self-criticism must balance receptiveness, or what was once
threatened with sterility merely grows flaccid.

—Am I still free of fear, and can I live truly in the times,
which are times of change and therefore demand change of the
instrument that would be serviceable for change?

—Do I balance a revolutionary will with a community will,
which stays with and works with others, in freedom from the
systems and slaveries that threaten to claim both me and others?

—Do I seek a subtle form of security, of vindication here and
now, at the price of healing and forgiveness? Or, on the other
hand, do I make a forgiving will into an excuse for allowing
injustice to go forward, in the secrecy which the system always
accords to injustice?

—Do I see myself as a symbol of change whose purity as a

symbol must remain untouched by the choices of others? Do I
seek a "consensus" which is no more than a moral accommoda-
tion, a slightly superior form of the old social lie, which has
become more palatable to those who accept revolution after it
has been paid for by others, who adopt new forms of life like
parasites? Am I a revolutionary *Vaincu,* in their company, allowing freedom to become a stereotype, in place of the continuing
struggle which marks real life? The point of my present life
being, not that I am suffering harassment for talking on an unpopular peace, the point being that the war in Viet Nam, with
its increasing horror and insensitivity to life, to world opinion,
to conscience, is going on in spite of all we can do—or more
exactly because we are not doing enough.

It seems as though this war is destined to become much more
decisive for me and for a few others than the civil rights
struggle had been. Most of us were not with this former struggle
with anything like the same intensity. We were not in jail, we
were not murdered or in exile, and most of us did not even
have friends who had so suffered. But during the war, we felt
that our turn would come too. It was our chance, one of the
unpalatable ironies of the present time. What was bringing
death to others was bearing a release of energies to us. It was
as though the death of the innocent were tapping our veins—or
better were offering us a blood transfusion. We could start, and
we might even catch up with events. We might bring "the good
news from Aix," as though a dawn, or a consciousness, had somehow arisen. Who knows? By being faithful to the sufferings of
the innocent, by being—by standing with them—we might even
have our own innocence restored. It was at least worth trying;
especially because there might not be another chance. We knew
that we had missed too many chances already.

"A feeling of reverence for that in man which is always trying
to outdistance itself" (Silone).

"In the face of revolting injustice, the only thing to do is to
revolt, and to leave introspection for better times." Except that
the better times may never arrive at all, and will almost certainly
not arrive in our lifetime. So we had better be introspective

along with our revolution, as a way of saving the revolution, and saving our minds to boot! Unless we wish to go from unconscious life to unconscious death.

What is my faith? In whom? Why? How deeply does it cut? It seems strange how the things we go through, if they are endured calmly and confidently, destroy us, destroy the forms of our faith. Events are like a wave of fire unfurling along a wild, rank growth of forest. The real growth has a chance to start only when the parasites are burned and toppled. And even good things become parasitic when life is struggling for new forms.

Faith becomes useless when it becomes a temptation to domesticate life itself—by identifying with others in too unquestioning a way, by becoming the shaman in the totem house instead of the initiator of faithful action in the world. By being enthusiastic, grandiose, paternalistic, cheaply pentecostal about the least gains in official concessions to human life, instead of remaining circumspect, exigent, with one's eyes opened both on church and world, mindful that church reform by churchmen, with no pressures from the world, is unimaginable and useless. A correct skepticism—about one's self, church, others, which is not corrosive or sick—but a point of contact. One has not agreed to rhetoric, even to sacred rhetoric, as a basis for life. He wants, believe it or not, the truth.

The uselessness of preempting a cause without necessary preparation—in conscience, in time, in prayer. Only by such a preparation can one be in his cause as he is in his own body, as he cannot imagine himself apart from the world. Apart from such preparation, only an absurd and pitiful betrayal of what one had briefly "stood for"—but only as a rootless tree stands, not because it is firmly in place, having grown there, but because no winds have struck it.

We have not yet really touched on the connection between worship and conscience. But it may be helpful to suggest that a lifetime of liturgy wrongly done, which is to say done without a passion for the living—a disconnected liturgy, one that advances from world to altar in profound and incorrigible ignorance, such a worship will be a positive obstacle to conscience, instead of its creator or midwife.

A man at times senses with a sinking feeling that he is incapable of love, while the truth of the matter may be that he is outgrowing conventional love. To be hardy and merciful, to grow in the power of exposure until one's body and spirit are as sensitive as an exposed part. The touchstone of Christ seems to offer this opening toward life. A heart which does not exist for itself, but which animates other hearts. This is one clue to the "super" language of Teilhard, a language which is satisfactory only to a degree, in describing the radiance which life must send out toward others if it is to be faithful to its own vocation.

"A personal testimony."

"But who wants your personal testimony?"

"I demand it of myself. I want to know why I am here. I want to know why I suffer. I cannot conceive of a life which is like an empty house, a blank stare outward. I want to be inhabited, a meeting place of spirits."

"Even of devils?"

"Yes. Better than a corpse. But the question is incomplete. Because where devils gather to possess a man, the angels gather too to defend him. They know that, when devils sense an opening, it is because a man is daring to live; the angels want to make the odds even. And Christ Our Lord knew, if not possession, at least what it means to be assailed. He knew that one cannot discriminate among spirits, in such a way as to stand entirely apart from evil. To be open to spirits is to be under siege by demons as well as by angels. And there is a kind of liberation in the thought. It may be that the angels teach one his strength. And the devils his weaknesses. And both are of the essence."

TRINIDAD

To exorcise our desolation, fear, and dread, it is necessary first to have gone to the depths of "drinking that cup." No cheap solutions to mysteries. Only a skill in living with mysteries.

Sometimes I am appalled to be able to share so little, and at such distance, in the reactions of others to cases of injustice. A terrifying somnolence seems to narcotize my emotional life. Does this mean I am indifferent to love, indifferent to the reality of justice? I hope not. The single guarantee I have that my hope is not illusory; while I cannot become seriously aroused at injustice done to myself, the same treatment accorded to others has a far different effect on me. I suddenly begin with a kind of exigent joy to be a man once more.

Our difficulty is not that commands are given to us. We have no quarrel with authority. We welcome it as an absolutely necessary completion of our souls, an invitation of the God whose love is always a summons, whose command creates freedom. Our protest is rather against commands that contain no mystery, that leave us deluded, empty, exhausted. Commands that presume to announce an epiphany, but grant us only a spectacle of fear or egoism in reaction. Such commands do not bestow on us the love of the Father, dislocating and difficult as that love must always be. They rather diminish our capacity for love, they stagger us like an unjust blow. And they are all the more pernicious because they demand our best response in the name of a God who our own instinct tells us is absent; who has in fact withdrawn from the scene.

The presence of God in the disponability of the one who commands means that he is not only ready to submit to the command he issues. Something far deeper is also implied. Such a man must love me, in whose direction the command is issued. He must know my strength and weakness, and take them into account. He must submit to conversion to the living God as must I; only in such a case can he speak for God. Often the integrity of his speech will be shown in simple trust. His conscience will be real and concrete. It will not disdain to respect even me as its testing ground. If I am real to authority, it is inevitable that commands will become real to me. And the opposite is equally true, and must be taken into account.

Someone suggests in public that my present sojourn in Latin America is good for me, that I need to learn gentleness; and

further that it is good for me as "one man dying for the people."
As to the first, I can only agree, although I am not entirely clear
on whether the present solution was devised in order to exorcise
my devils. On the second point, I am somewhat unclear as to
the appropriateness of quoting a Jewish high priest as an authority for Christian conduct. Perhaps. In a different context, it is
said that our Lord died for many, and I can take an unworthy
and minimal part in that economy. We repeat these words day
after day at the Mass. It is probably no more than right to be
required to put up some surety on the words from time to time.

GUIANA

What others love, what awakens friendship, is not a search for
understanding by others, or even an attempt, however unselfish,
to understand others. The first can be a form of sensuality, the
second of arrogance. But in friendship, purely and maturely
understood, one seeks precisely nothing at all. Nothing that is
except the exercise of an instinct which is not a consciousness of
one's self as virtue or power, but a tendency toward others. Not
a mechanism but a process. What we love when we love is the
inestimable privilege of having some part in another's destiny
—indeed, of being integral to it. Not merely an enlargement of
consciousness which slowly includes others. But even more. A
hunger and thirst of spirit which only others can assuage. My
spirit is an explorer.

How many crimes in the world would be averted by the power
of example, if believers would resolve, not let us say through
fidelity to their Lord (this is perhaps asking too much) but in
fidelity to the simple moral hope of other good men—if they
would resolve not to approve murder or bless the destroyers of
men. Believers might begin then a momentous act by turning
to other men simply as men. The results of such preliminary
practice would be extraordinary, for believers as well as for
others. But the probability of such an occurrence is not great.
The world, as a consequence, will not be Christian until Christians have evolved into human beings.

Disappearance from a scene which alone has allowed the

meaning of one's existence to emerge in and for others. And again, the pondering of heart which is stimulated by the death of a man. All our absences are in some measure an image of the great gift which death offers to men. It allows them to seize on and to interiorize the meaning of the lives of others. Tragedy, absurdity, injustice, when they occur, are greatly important and a great gift. They help release death from its aspect of sweat and struggle, and raise it to the plane of serenity and spiritual conquest—a choice, an invitation to which one is privileged to respond.

"We are not so mad as to think that we shall create a world in which murder will not occur. We are fighting for a world in which murder will no longer be legal" (Camus).

To eat and drink the world, not in the old, forbidden sense of rebellion. But tasting the world as a chalice of the Father, tasting that beloved community, in its bitterness and loss and alienation, in its beginnings, its fits and starts, its idealism and crime. That from such meat and drink one's heart may beat a day longer. Not as an integer added to others, not as combatant or a source of coercion, or as another destroyer. But to breathe spirit on others, to serve. One who, being seen, gives hope. Perhaps only for a day longer. Indeed, one day may consummate a life: "What made us dream that he would comb gray hair?" (Yeats)

CARACAS

I have been reading Isaias in preparation for Christmas: "Do not fear, I have ransomed you. I have called you by your name, you are mine. If you pass through the waters, I will be with you; through great waves, they will not overwhelm you. If you pass through fires they will not burn you, the flames will not consume you. For I am God, the Holy One of Israel, your God." Trying humbly and realistically to understand such assurances, in lands where hope is either a cheap commodity for the rich, or is simply absent, like a sufficiency of food for the starving. And being removed from a community where hope was assured day and night by those around me, by a new season, by a language of gentleness and trust. So much absurdity, so much injustice, so little preparation for crisis surely puts hope to an iron test. And yet to know in one's deepest heart that one is required to hope on more strongly than others, to purify his consciousness to the point where he can hope for those even who are without hope, even when one is inarticulate and helpless before their despair. To hope as well for the absent. To hope for peace as though one were free to work for peace, with others who had trusted and whom one may even have awakened. To hope for a future; not by evasion, but because one has been denied a present time to work in. To trust that our God, who has obscurely been at work in all of this, has not, in denying one his valid part in present life, has not forbidden the future, or canceled one's efforts, or cut one off from hope. To trust even those who have shown themselves incapable of trust, or have broken the bonds of mutual trust. To do what one can, in his own thoughts, to heal and bind up, to forgive, to abjure self-pity, to remain strong and resourceful. To remain capable of love in the least promising circumstances. To remain grateful and unvictimized by the times.

"The first happenings; behold they have already occurred. I foretell new ones; before they occur, I proclaim them" (Isaias 42 : 9).

The lifetime search for freedom, which cannot be carried on apart from others and which must be paid for, and heavily.
The futility of a freedom which consists only in self-vindication. Which goes on at distance from the Cross.

We have not been able so far to make contact here with people one could consider revolutionary in a Gospel sense. Even those who are working among the poor are doing so with no real understanding of what underlies the injustices they are attempting to solace. No one has gone so far into the roots of injustice as have the priest workers, for example. The orders are "lending out" one or another man from the main work, which is in effect an irrelevant work—this or that school, this or that structure. We met today with two priests who are struggling in Ebario pretty much alone. Their work may come to something in time.

But the main attack on structures of privilege is yet to come. One movement is subsisting on charity, working among the poor. But the fabric of economy is rotten—whole areas, mile after mile of families, are entirely out of economic hope. One wonders whether the Church can claim here to be anything but a defender and purveyor of the status quo—a terrifying thought, considering what must lie to the south of us.

The photos we have seen at certain centers show the old church pattern. A bishop blesses the rich patrons who come to "do something" for the poor out of their bounty. A bright spot is the three American girls from the Peace Corps and "Accion" living in the Barrio, and loving it. But who is questioning their presence, and whether they are also blessing a system which must eventually, by one means or another, be changed or toppled?

Violence—justified "because groups of men are convinced they are masters of the universe. But this passage into possession leads through one's own body" (Simone Weil). A powerful reason, therefore, to dispense with violence is simply that one is defending himself against violence. He does not want such a passage opened; much less does he want it to become a public domain. From another point of view, the opening toward a better life demands legitimately that one becomes subject to spiritual change. And this is suffering indeed; but it alone can prepare for a possession of the world which is not destructive of others and of one's self.

"To prove something"—a most sterile and useless of tasks. Whereas great lives prove precisely nothing. They are, from the Cartesian point of view, useless. What life truly seeks, when it is being led at depth, is fidelity to actual times. A response and invitation which is at the same time profoundly submissive.

Consider the lag in conscience of one who first of all is most exact in "religious observance," for whom "the Mass is everything," and yet whose public actions are marked by unawakened resolve or by positive injustice. One would be horrified at the suggestion of sacrilege at the altar; at the same time one is

ready for sacrilege against his neighbor. Indeed the possibility
of the second does not occur to such a man under the sign of
danger of sin. And when such sin has actually occurred, in the
judgment of witnesses, it can be rather easily dismissed.

And then there is the question of a somnolent conscience,
which never objectively awakens beyond the capacities of childhood. One walks through a world of living men as though one
trod on sticks and stones.

Today we cry "Church! Church!" somewhat as the men of
our Lord's time cried out "Lord! Lord!" But the cries are equally
unavailing when a man's works are dead.

I would like every soldier to be of such mind that, though
fully in love with life, he would rather be killed than kill. I
would like every churchman who blesses war or is silent during
war to be conscious to the same degree of the same priorities.
Such a rule deserves the name golden; it is rare indeed. And I
find that only the poor are rich in its possession. Having suffered
violence, they are able in a kingly and prophetic way, which is
also supremely moving, to renounce violence. And they, if anyone can do so, will lead us into the same light.

Some men have the privilege of voyaging to the edge of inherited life. They work there and they profoundly dislocate the
center and edges by leading other men to the same work of
transformation. And this is indeed a great thing. But an even
greater thing is to die at the edge, adding to the witness of
communion and unselfishness that of the Cross. A historical

death in the truest sense. One whose silence is an imperious
appeal to a future one was not allowed to see. To die in this
way is to guarantee a *sur croit de vie* for others by being despoiled
one's self. A resurrection—but an act of God, not a human vindication. The importance of dying as one has lived, so that the
end in a noble sense may justify the means.

VIII

MANAUS

THE DESOLATE sense recurs like an incoming tide. The sense of being a source of disunity when one had hoped to create and sustain unity. A great sorrow, perhaps the only one worth talking about. "That out of many hearts, thoughts may be revealed." And how they are revealed! In a flood of panic and retribution and thoughtless violence.

To search out the intelligibility of what one is undergoing, so that the mystery may be isolated and seen for what it is. To admit the presence of human failure and malice. Not for the sake of self-vindication, but to serve the mystery. God, who is not afraid to be at the use of man, does not easily consent to be misused by him. Recurrence to the vow of obedience in order to mask injustice is an act of irreligion. Likewise, submission to injustice, or ignoring its presence, is a connivance in the same sin.

We do not seek justice as a final good. Or if we do, we never succeed in getting beyond mere justice. But we seek justice in order, first of all, to be just men; and, secondly, in order to be treated justly—and all this for the sake of love. But we cannot ignore the first and yet claim the second.

The terrifying durability of injustice in history. We read the past with a measure of righteousness and condemn those who condemned Christ or Socrates or Joan of Arc. But most of us would condemn the same innocent ones today if their cases lay before us. Which is to say, we are capable normally of justice only toward the dead. But the innocence and greatness of the living are too much for us. The evidence, we like to say, is not all in—an admission that justice, and its kingdom, can never come to pass in time. And of course they never can, in the persecutor. Only in the victim.

To draw the mysteries of God away from their human soil is to kill the mysteries as far as true understanding goes. Still, one must distinguish the plant from its soil, even while he lives on the fruit that grows from the soil. Divine love, flowering from human life—even from human mire. And the mystery of man must be compounded with the same soil—in life and death. To pluck the fruit is to die a little, even while one lives more vigorously from eating the fruit.

BELEM

Without mail delivery, having to imagine my friends' lives, looking at a watch to help imagine what they are doing at this time of Christmas. A strange, levitated time, deprived of the faces of those I love, of their voices, of the unexplainable beauty and terror of wartime, of evening gatherings, of the Eucharist celebrated with those I love. Like a land animal taught to survive in water, never loving the water. A strange suspension of life, a sense of waste, a wasting anger, the struggle to stand with feet planted in past and future, as though these alone existed, since the present seems a blank. The phantoms crowd in on the vacuum —they seek a settlement out of court of what they call their fate; which is, in fact, my own. Illegitimate decisions—choices of love, of hatred, of refusal, and of combat. Choices which cannot be made at present, since all that is asked now is stillness, the stillness of a vortex, borne about by winds not of my own raising, in directions I have not chosen, for purposes I can neither understand nor interpret.

The reason for all this is absurd. It is the question of a drowned man, a question asked under water. The secret is to drown the search for reasoning in acceptance; in those lives among whom I move, allowing their lives to impinge on mine; in their sadness and nobility, their sense of place, their roots which can never be mine. What a short time, what a long time! A time of exile, which goes by other clocks than time in community, than time of trust and love and labor. I shall never be the same man again. I look at the crucifix on my desk and I try, in measure, to understand. A shape which has accompanied me everywhere, on all the trips that once had such purpose and clarity. A talk to give, an audience waiting, friends, those who opposed me. The time when my mind was in service and stretched itself to the utmost, a sail that bore a whole company of others along with me. Now I am fastened down. To an obedience as hard as it is inhuman; to injustice.

The cross, the disordered, tempestuous, purposeful world—a disposition, a dispensation. At its noblest, interpreted by an intellect that accepted the cross because beyond and within it lay the mystery of the Father's will. Unbearable by human resources—not as an instrument of blood but as an instrument of injustice. Bearable, even longed for, embraced, as a sign. I accept, even with half a heart.

RECIFE
"The hand of Jahweh is on that mountain; he has stretched out his hand, as a swimmer stretches out his hand to swim" (Isaias 25 : 11).   .

To conclude a peace treaty too quickly with one's self is to fall into the unresolved hatred which one has neither conquered nor truly understood. One was merely victimized by a false peace of his own making.

One of the worst illusions of all: that change comes about by intellectual means alone. Change in men is wrought by men. It has to do with new attitudes toward freedom, responsibility, and love, which awaken neither as pure ideas nor as unrealized values. Interminable intellectualism is a curse; it cuts off all newness in this direction. Not only does 90 percent of it lead in the wrong path; it also actually persuades men that to put off their real efforts in favor of analysis, abstraction, and theorizing is the main task. Yet from the New Testament to the Civil Rights movement, we find something entirely different at work. Men judge clearly and initiate new ways of change, ways that place their lives in the front lines of risk, labor, danger, and suffering. Yet we pluck talented men from the world which is moving in this way, amortize their capacities, plunge them into theories of social change which are almost exclusively artistic or intellectual. As a result, protests against injustice, a sense of the wrongs suffered by minority peoples, a thirst for justice, are extremely rare among us. The mortal danger that strikes talented

men with a particular force is the conviction that human life
can be fulfilled in such a way.

To sense one's incapacity and to preserve, at least obscurely,
capacities for grace. "The infinite pretensions of our evil, together with their limited energy."

To seize the present for the uses of grace, especially when
the present is an emptiness, marked by distaste, even by disgust,
for those with whom one works, together with a seemingly
endless incapacity for love.

To accept one's wretchedness without being victimized by it
—the difference between Christ and the devil. A wretchedness
which can be the starting point not only of moral beauty but of
art and insight as well.

RIO

The act of faith substitutes space for time. One can live in
the present, being summoned to do so, ignoring the threats of
the future and of the past, because the present is of significance,
revealed to one in those he loves and works with.

Life here, in the face of the tragedy of the floods, seems so
neutral and colorless. One has so little to say before the spectacle
of death. So little to write; one's reflections seem empty and
pointless. One reason may be the stasis that always accompanies
tragedy. The window dressing seems to have been stripped
away. Very little of life remains subject to doubt or debate
before the faces of the dead. Even tactics and plans on behalf
of peace seem to be supremely unreal. One is left with a feeble,
insecure form of intercessory prayer.

Can the slave redeem the master? Never, so long as he is a
slave. But suppose he has become a free man, constrained under
a power which may presume to be total, but which is in fact
less than human, fixed, chancy, the response of a stricken animal,
the unpredictable absurdity of accident or disease, a calamity
in nature? This is how fear reacts to a threat; it can never be
the way for human beings. But how does one treat with men

who act so immorally that they seem to stand at the side of those without faith and without human resources? To treat with such men as a common disaster in nature is perhaps a first instinct. But however such men may have reverted to a predatory level, they remain our brothers. One can be crushed by a convention of small minds endowed with too great a burden of power. Or one can be destroyed as he steps onto the street before a drunken driver. He is in no sense accountable for the madman at the wheel; but for the other men, he is.

The Church, we say, is apostolic. She draws continuously the interest and principal from her first gift. She is in fact both bearer and substance of the love which gave her existence. But perhaps one would have to have suffered something in order to wrestle with another aspect of this gift. Continuity in evil, as well as in goodness. The life line which evil, as well as goodness, unskeins in time. So a question arises, which takes on all the moral urgency of a temptation; which, after all, is more tenacious, more careful to assure its well-being, more skilled in creating children to its own image—evil or goodness? And if goodness and love define the Church, then how explain the massive, stony resistance which greets a call to change? Is it truly a gift to be so old on the earth if one's energy is spent in resisting youth?

Against big claims: We are, after all, beset and ignorant men, whose number includes a certain percentage of unusually intelligent and compassionate men—perhaps more, perhaps less than other professions around us. We serve a mystery which owes very little to us—and the majority of us serve it badly. Apart from moods of fervor and occasions of insight, we find our place and submit to it with habits of mind and routines of thought which normally do not drive us very deep. We are shaken into a sense of life with as much difficulty as the majority of those around us. All this is not to puncture our ministry with cynicism or naturalism. It is only to underscore what each of us knows in his deepest heart. We are unprofitable servants whose first requirements of soul are not always met—obedience to the reality of our lives. In the light of this need, clericalism, big words, triumphalism, professional apartness, appear more clearly for what they are. But the hope is that such things may now be subject to exorcism, surely a form of renewal.

IX

SAO PAULO

A MEETING with the worker-priests. How is it that these men awaken in my heart a relish for the Church which springs up again despite all that seems at the moment most destructive and devouring: injustice, long periods of misunderstanding, the pain of meeting with forms of power that seem determined to banish justice, joy, largeness of spirit into outer darkness? I walk into their poor rooms and visit their church, and look around me with a delight, the misbelieving, half-hoping, half-denying leap of hope which a slum child must know at the sight of a sudden smile—surprised by joy. I did not know the world or life or my life could be like this. Neither did I know the Church could be like this—or I had forgotten it, or neglected to recall it, although I had known the same experience with these men in Paris. One had come almost to believe that rightist politics, rational bias, favor of the powerful and rich, that these were winning out. Or one was sick at heart and resigned to losing, to being alone, or very nearly so. And suddenly—in no more space than a step from a fouled street into a garden—one knows: The Gospel works; one is again at the center of things, the show can go on with all its pettiness; one can bear with it because he has found a center of gravity, a center of grace. I am intoxicated with this sudden healing, which asked so little of the sick man, which gave so completely of its meek, welcoming power. Like the impact of pure and genuine art, of friendship, of the simplest offering of love, which has no need to strive for argument or effect or to prove a point, but which gathers life to itself, purifying and transforming. The Church may even be this. It may yet be a giver of life in giving itself to life. It may put down roots and offer fruits to man's despair. I believe, and my credo takes this form—the form of men who believe.

BUENOS AIRES

We first encountered here a word of the twenty-seven priests of Mendoza. I find their letter to the bishops of Brazil very moving, honest, and direct. A loss of a sense of the sacred often implies that one has fled the demands of the sacred. Another aspect: the neglect of justice toward the neighbor. The signs that such a movement may be of the Holy Spirit: (1) The continuation of their life of community and of prayer; (2) The effort to localize obedience at its center rather than to "spiritualize" it out of human responsibility; (3) A willingness to suffer concretely at the hands of men, in order to bring a more authentic unity to the Church.

> . . . We ask that the problems of Argentina (and we are convinced that this is a national problem which should be treated as such) be once and for all faced with realism and truth. We believe there is no other way to restore the values of authority, which has so deteriorated in these last days. May the good name of Christ and the sacred realities we are privileged to serve be not misused to serve personal interests. No one has a monopoly on the Lord. No one, no matter how high his ministry, can assume the judicial power of one Judge. Before a ministry of suffering and of the cross, we ask that no one assume the privilege of being the only victim. All are suffering; we as well as others. We who know we are sinners, know also that we are capable of equivocating. We know that we can be mistaken, that we are far from perfect. But we know too that we have been forced to take these extreme steps, when for many years, all other ways have been closed against us. We accept once again the decision of the Holy See, to which we have had recourse. We repeat our conviction that this is an hour of suffering, and an hour of grace as well. An hour in which the Spirit is breathing in His Church. An hour of which we are unworthy, but which God has seen fit to confer upon us, and in which we beseech of God the grace not to be unfaithful.

SALTA

Is it enough to be innocent? I think not. Innocence must justify itself against the guilt that masks as innocence. Sometimes time and human change will be the justifying forces. But we cannot be sure, and cannot merely wait, since the innocence of others is also assailed, and waits for us.

To reduce the ambiguities of nonviolence to an inner clarity.

Thus; not to oppose evil with violence is a far different thing than not to oppose evil. But when does silence before evil become connivance with evil? I do not know.

The accordion quality of time. Its constriction into moments which become a form of active temptation, fine tongues of fire which declare, "You cannot bear this." Likewise, the enticing expansion of life into moments which seem to promise, here and now, paradise. To be trapped by neither. To understand that each is inevitable, and that neither is definitive. The two faces of time—which is to say, of personality, of one's self.

Evasion: to count ahead in time of suffering, to a time of no suffering or, at least, of relief from this suffering. A leap to which imagination summons one; friends, congenial atmosphere, renewal of community. The lure is the prospect of a leap. But time itself demands that we go step by step, a path which is all too evidently beneath our feet.

If only other men would change! Which is to say: If only I were not required to change. Or, more exactly, if I were not required to die. But love of life itself, as contrasted with love of illusion, requires this death.

Living with the event of death, the death of the innocent, of friends, of the young, the terribly difficult and opaque death by immolation, from which so many recoiled in horror. The only way is by way of consent, in all these deaths, to the death of one's self. To allow that precious part of one's life—these sharings never to be repeated; these faces and voices to die, to recede, to live on no more in this world. To consent to death as the culmination of life itself, as a promise of new life, as the release of eternal life, as the full flowering of that beauty one has rejoiced in. By successive deaths, consented to, embraced, one becomes less unworthy of life, of the promise of Christ—"abundantius."

A refusal of extravagant inner gestures of elation or of discouragement. The false fruits of a false paradise which the rigorous Gospel neither promises nor confers. Not stoicism, either, as alternative, but a modest Christianity.

The claims of the Church should echo in content and method the claims of Christ. And His are so gentle, so near to silence, so willing to let life speak for itself. So conscious of history—not only of its sin but also of its false promises.

The revolution of twenty years ago becomes the reaction of today. So one is driven to defend what once seemed self-evident, luminous, instinctively right and needful. But because the law intervened, or a visionary grew old and became obsessed with a project—the casting of his vision in bronze.

Truly to meet one's times, and to invite others to meet them, forbids one to try to meet all the future. Except by the most delicate and conscious invitation issued to free men to discover new forms of their freedom. The bones of founders should be burned.

It is one thing to say; "I am determined to express and share my freedom in new forms, in new communities." It is quite another thing to invite other men to do the same thing. But the *una sancta fides* rigorously includes both processes.

To be truly delivered from evil. Not by a *deus ex machina,* but by grace, which is no deliverance at all, no tug of the wires but a prevailing of the will toward service.

One hopes to understand in this world perhaps one percent of his experience, his suffering, his sin. For the rest, he pays a tribute to mystery. He chooses not to know more, not to attempt to speak of more.

The arrival of the kingdom of justice, even in its minimal requirements of respect and love and justice—is this too great a hope for this world, or for the Church? When the Kingdom seems to be indefinitely delayed, it may be because one has not yet acceded to its coming within himself. In the effort to be more faithful, in the fidelity to what stands before one here and now—burdensome and clamorous as it is—one understands the smallness and greatness of that claim which is the echo of the Gospel: "the least of these, my brethren."

"Now that I am an adult, I put away the things of a child." But do I? Changes of mode, changes of locale, even of weather, induce so often a change of heart—languid, depressed, stewing about in reverie or illusion or dreams of better times. One learns through his wretchedness that the "putting away" is not so simple as closing a cupboard of toys. It consists in dealing adequately with one's past, and the insistence of the past in taking part in what one is becoming now, for good or for ill.

"I entered into a life I was not fitted for" seems to me the last whimper of the romantic. "I entered into life, and fitted my soul to the shape of life itself." The cry of a man determined that his soul shall contain and express the world itself.

SALTA

The difficulties of "establishing an apostolate." But what is implicitly in question is not apostolate, but a new form of the establishment. The people are not heard, their needs are largely unknown, the bricks are imported. It is a kind of exact and ironic antiplay on the Incarnation. And it has two sources in the imagination: (1) Claims that are too large to be true, and therefore impossible to meet; the depersonalizing of "the way" into a code; a conviction, immensely strong and deeply ingrained, that one speaks for God and announces His will. And (2) Ignorance of the world; that is, a distrust of experience as a guide to action. A view of the future which is no more than the updating and repairing and extension of old forms. In this vacuum, in its density and protectionism, all sorts of illusions flourish; a kind of mushroom cellar. By way of contrast, one notes the need of (1) modest language about one's self and one's work; efforts to stress active charity as a religious attitude, a language that is not a stranger to the Gospel; its simplicity and willingness to learn from others. And (2) love of the world, a field of force whose vibrations strike the heart with resonances that are both recognition and invitation.

Perhaps when the mourning for modern atheism is finished, it may become clearer that men do not want our God. But such men are not generally heard from, and those who question us with a seriousness that could form a basis for mutual enlightenment are forced to construct their own gods, or to live and die with no gods at all.

We saw yesterday an old priest in his soutane, passing slowly through the streets, leaning on his stick; no one spoke to him, he looked at no one; he seemed remote as a bonze, taken for granted, simply part of the landscape. Then later, two old nuns shuffled along in the Sunday crowds. Church renewal, new theology, had left them as untouched as the dead in the hillside cemetery. It would be easy to dismiss all this as a mere cultural curiosity. We are often harsh and blasé in our judgments. But what do these lives mean, in the great vessel of prayer and dedication that fills the world to its brim, that startles us from faces hardly touched by the blows of this world, that allows us the hope of a gentler judgment than we deserve?

Clouds of butterflies surrounded the airliner as we came into the city. They melted past the great wings, borne on the air stream like a storm of flowers. We had never seen anything like it. Then yesterday we drove fifty miles into the mountains, and the butterflies again, moving in one direction on the winds, broken on the windshield in airy patches like stars, that dried and glittered in the sunshine.

The innocence and inventiveness of the dancers. There seems to be no activity that so seizes on a man, twisting him into new and ever newer forms, so that even his clothing seems to go up in flame. And then it is finished—in a way in which no poem is ever finished. The most unselfish of the arts, which consumes itself in its own giving.

The difficulties of a trip such as this one, patched together so suddenly, without serious preparation—in a way, an epitome of the "sending Church." The abrasions of life together, our moods, our thoughtlessness. The stifling sense of being unable to dig deeply into the lives and scenes we come upon. The sense of wasting time, of adding nothing of light or heat to men who themselves are caught; in the wrong place, with the wrong work, seeing little or no way out. The sense of being inarticulate before suffering. One ends most days with a sense of weary frustration, a ground, as one knows, both for faith and for despair. A faith for which one is totally unprepared and unworthy, a despair for which one is all too ready and eager. The shock of forever moving on, the almost constant presence of a creeping undiscipline, a sense of ennui and disgust with the Church—*cui bono?* And then, too, the springs in the desert, rare and beautiful; a meeting with men who are marked by suffering and endurance. A sense that somehow the enterprise is winning through, that the enterprise is worthwhile, that love is available. A sense of waiting and listening, a taste for mystery reasserting itself against all evidence. The faces of the young or the very old, expressing the *numen loci,* that the earth has meant to man—toil, fidelity, the cost of joy. And one's suffering takes on a truer aspect, more balance and perspective. One's life may have no mark of greatness about it, but neither is it entirely wretched or absurd. It is redeemed by communion, the possibility of love that is both obscure and undeserved.

The point at which one can do nothing—the point of truth.

To verbalize, or "express," the faith becomes increasingly difficult and perhaps increasingly useless. But perhaps something better is possible—now and again to act faithfully for others.

Submission before injustice creates unjust men as its victims, a bitterness which is at great distance from the limpidity of the "Gospel eye." So the man of justice prevails only if his justice is stronger than that of the scribes and Pharisees.

One says to himself after a while (and to the world as well): "Believe it or not, I believe."

MENDOZA

The opposite of the "armed man who keeps his camp" is not the weakling who keeps (that is, is responsible for) nothing at all. It is the man of meekness, who keeps, not a fortress like a *défi* in the face of God, but gently, gently, by the power of his moral reach and grasp, the world itself. Which is to say, he keeps the natural equivalent and extension of his own heart.

This evening we came in by plane in choppy, vicious weather, all the more deceptive and dangerous because the winds fought us in a clear and brilliant air whose eye seemed to disclaim any double-dealing. And midway in, one (of only two extant) motor failed us. The plane dipped and swam sidelong, like a whale with a stricken fluke. And I was too sick to look up, and took the whole thing for another jolt in the storm. And so we landed, green as whey and ignorant as a stone. Which is perhaps the ignominious way that death comes—as one distraction among many, one more senseless buffeting.

The truest wretchedness is to be ignorant of one's wretchedness. Which puts these weeks perhaps in a more hopeful light—since during them one has come to know his condition to the hilt. Naked as a skinned animal, out of one's element, tempted to despair of the future. And in debt with a double indemnity: having encountered the worst and undergone it; and then on the road being exposed to such appalling suffering all around us, the dead ends of human lives, the shaking of lives to the very seams. Without and within, so little left, so little to be made of such rags and remnants. Which may after all be a kind of biblical scene. For we witnessed in ourselves the death of the medicine man, the breaking of his bottles, the waste and loss of his useless medicines. And then perhaps, in this bitter vacuum, the approach of the awesome Healer himself.

During most of the time of his life, it is not apparent that a man may be living with a corrupt heart, that his metal may be debased. For life is not continually probing us, any more than doctors are. It is only crisis that tries us to our marrow and, in the nature of things, crisis is rare. But woe to the man of weakness, and woe to the man whose weakness threatens others, and double woe to those who are dependent on such a man. They may well go down with him. Still, on the other hand, the crisis we speak of may be saving as well as destructive. And the deepest trouble of all may not be a question of false men, but the question of false hope. And to be rid of that hope is a great liberation indeed—so great that most men can only fear it.

Is it unfair or unfaithful to judge religion by the kinds of lives it creates? Perhaps the judgment can be applied usefully only if it is applied with moderation. Some men would be knaves or weaklings or bigots, even if God were incarnate under their roof. Others are magnanimous, self-sacrificing, even without an admitted faith in God. All of which is only to repeat a truism: Man is free and unfree at once, victimized by his illusions, by egoism, by inheritance. But he is also capable of walking toward the light, and of embracing it with his whole being, and of being transformed into a "son of light." And this is his glory, and the reason why the light has descended to us, and become "the light of the world." Whence, too, the apologetic of the luminous Christian, and the scandal offered by the unconverted Christian —a darkness masquerading as light—source, in fact, of a double darkness, a Christianity that brings no change to pass.

Nonviolence, in its implicit will to accept other men as they are, is always open to the charge of temporizing and of cowardice. But it is, in fact, the only historical realism worth talking about, paying tribute as it does to the action of spirit upon spirit, the change that operates through presence, example, communion, and the gift of one's self.

"Each time a plane releases its bombs on a Vietnamese village, killing its women and children, a bomber which is operated by a white Westerner, one of the sonorous phrases of the Vatican Council goes up in smoke. I am not a conscientious objector; and I weigh my words" (Head of International Caritas).

I sit in my room, overlooking a beautiful, tended garden in

which the priests walk, making their prayer in the sunlight. A
school is conducted here, some 150 students taught by 15 priests.
Outside the walls, the tumultuous life and noise of the city, one
of the most vital in this country. About 5 percent of the people
practice the faith. Thus far the facts without. Within, a Fran-
ciscan or Trappist scene. A certain gentle rhythm, lives that
continue inheriting and inhabiting structures that are profoundly
unreal before the needs of the times, but that are scarcely ever
questioned. We have seen the same scene repeated, almost like a
photo multiplied, in city after city of Latin America. The Church
swallowed whole by the past.

SANTIAGO

What could imaginably be more sterile than an act of faith
that has not passed through the imagination?

When one finds his loyalties placed in question, it may be
because, for the first time, his loyalties are striking bedrock. It
may be so, and it may not be so. The reason may also be that
one has ceased to have any loyalties at all. The only criterion
I know is one's willingness to suffer and stand with others.

A man is busy probing another's weakness; when will he have
heart for another's strength?

The real meaning of the "domino theory"—the future falls
when the present is corrupted. Every war is the guarantee of
future war. Contrast: "Purify the means!" (Gandhi)

The time for peacemaking is exactly when the peace is being
assailed. Pope Paul: "War never again!" The domino law in
action: "We agree, but after this war!"

After two months, and four letters which never arrived with
the news, at length the announcement of death, the piecing
together of the terrible story. The death by asphyxiation of three
friends in Mexico City. One of them, smiling, serene, and gently
thoughtful, had met me at the airport on that leaden evening
when my journey had begun, and the future had seemed so
bleak. In the days that followed, it would have been impossible
to imagine a greater courtesy at one's side. And this seemed to

me all the more wonderful and even disconcerting, since she had not known the events that had brought me to Latin America. But with her, the spirit was quick and alert, almost extrasensory. So my trip, which had begun with joy and confidence because of her, comes to its close under the sign of death. An irreplaceable beauty of mind is lost to us; a light is quenched. And when I seek to know how I have been affected, it seems to me that her death is joined in an abrupt and mysterious way, to the endurance by Christians of times of upheaval, of the wounds inflicted by a Church which so often has failed the human heart. Yet such men and women go on, living lives of radiant usefulness and service to others. She would not call herself a Catholic, although she had graduated from a Catholic college and had practiced the faith until the age of twenty-five or so. Then a crisis in her life was dealt with maladroitly by an unfeeling priest from whom she had sought help. But her life continued nonetheless, steadily and to all appearances peaceably. She served in the slums of Caracas for two years, and then went on to Mexico City to help in the relocation of poor families in the John Kennedy community then being built. In every sense, her life was before her. She was intelligent, winning, and courageous. She lived a disciplined life of personal solitude. The waters of her mind ran deep. She had few intimate friends, and was working her way intellectually and emotionally through the sufferings that had left so painful a scar. Hers was a faith of adventure and travail. Her bonds with the poor were strong and compassionate. One sensed that, with time, the God who remained so painfully hidden would show Himself in an epiphany dawning out of her life of service—a God who was joined bone and marrow with the poor to whose hope she had joined her own. Time was what she needed; there would be time enough. Or so we thought. Actually, there was very little time for her; there was to be only eternity. Faith, which had been her heaviest burden, was to be lifted from her shoulders forever.

Is it strange that I think of Abbé Godin, dead in his youth, just as the Mission de France was launched, dead also by asphyxiation in the cruel winter of Paris? A great work is not in man's hands. If it is to bear fruit, it must be of God. And it is in death that God asserts the law that was promulgated in his Son—no life without death; no new beginnings for men without the shedding of blood, without innocent suffering, and the coming of man to a dead end.

When I pray for her and for her brother and mother who died with her, my spirit lifts once more, "so great a sweetness flows." Some problems are so vexing and complicated that only death can solve them. A new existence is demanded by the derangement and injustice and anguish of this one. The Church, for all its sins, knows. And speaks well: "The life of the just is not taken away; it is changed for the better."

OSORNO

The land reform, the program of alphabetization are touchstones of revolution. So Frei is promoting both; so is Castro. And in Brazil, those who are working in these projects in jail or in exile. The reasoning on either side is obvious: To give man land, to teach him to read, is to give him roots and to deepen his consciousness. Both together make a hopeless man into a person. They mark him with thought and possession; they make possible creation and pride of place. To be on the land is also, in the Christian sense, something very different from the position of the landowners who enslave the peons and neglect the land itself. Such men, literate and cosmopolite, have holdings that exhaust the sun's range and yet they are baptized inhumans. And we have seen the same thing verified in the case of the poor: men with no possessions, who are as far from the Gospel Beatitude pronounced on the poor as they are from human development. No one inherits the Gospel who is totally disinherited from the earth—any more than possession of the land guarantees cleanness of heart.

From the plane, I can look down on small, neat land parcels, verdant and prosperous in the mild weather. They stand like endless gardens between the Andes and the sea. A reminder of our Midwest wheat basket, but with a difference. Here there are no dwellings spaced among the fields as a sign of ownership. Instead, at wide intervals, a miserable clutch of huts, and then a vast park and mansion. The fundo system; on the one hand no land, no culture, and no future. On the other, no conscience and a rapacious consciousness. In both cases, across centuries of neglect and secret frenzy, there stands the undeclared violence of underdevelopment—the thorn in the luxurious flesh, the dream of retribution long nursed, soon to be launched.

One understands a little better after Argentina and Chile the ancient promise of land after captivity. A promised land! But the land could be wrested from the possessor only at the price of war and murder. The old covenant could not be sealed so long as the people were landless. How can we preach the Gospel today to the disenfranchised, the unrepresented? We cannot, of course. We only imagine we can—the truest source of our illusion being our own covenant sealed with the powers of this world, in despite of the covenant of Christ's blood. We (and the powerful) will retain possession, and together will preach to the poor— either contentment and resignation under injustice (nineteenth-century spirituality) or contentment with false justice; which is to say, with moral and spiritual disintegration (twentieth-century spirituality). In the one case, loss of the immigrant poor; in the other, loss of the workers. And in both cases—loss by ourselves, preachers and powers, of the knowledge of God in this world. The Church being (clumsily) what God would have done with time, time being consciousness enlightened by His word and empowered to do His work.

Contrast the passionate desire of the *campesinos* to learn to read and write, and the refusal of some Harlem children to learn the same process—their instinctive recoiling from the white man's efforts to educate them. Efforts which they see as another tactic of occupation.

LIMA

Does man have a future? You have almost to be pushed to answer *no* before you can be ready really to say *yes*. I mean a yes that includes and surpasses all the noes—not merely hypothetically or possibly, but the noes that stifle the heart with their danger, their rightness, their logic, their malevolence and strength. The noes would include the judgment that man does

not deserve a future. That he does not want a future. That he
fears a future. That he wishes desperately and cunningly to
survive, and that, in order to survive he is quite willing to destroy
others. That his style and attitude within actual life are just
proof that he is unworthy of a future. One must know all the
arguments in order to see not only their logic and persuasiveness,
but also all that they have left unconsidered. Which is to say,
that power, the transforming power of spirit, the principle not
only of survival but of supererogation and plentitude. I have to
include the noes spoken against man in order to say *yes* to man.
I mean a yes that is plenary and effective, that brings to pass
what it affirms. To have heard in one's dark blood—Buchenwald,
Hiroshima, Little Rock, the Viet Nam horror—and still to say *yes*
to man. To give a no, not as one hears it in his inner ear, not
as spoken by others, by the enemies of mankind—but a no which
one has learned all too well, which expresses one's own soul as
he stands in revulsion before others. I mean, finally, to say *yes*
through a mysterious power that can never be finally claimed
or rationalized; a power that deals with evil in the world, that
has first dealt with evil in my own heart.

Human indignity attains another meaning here, and inevitably,
by way of contrast, men give another meaning to human dignity
than we are used to. How can those who honor themselves allow
others to be dishonored? We saw, coming in from the airport, the
smoldering, stinking *favellas*—half garbage heap, half dump—
where thousands of families live what may, with a kind of satanic
jocoseness, be called life. "And he fed the pigs, and would wish
to have eaten the husks of pigs" (St. Luke). "Man, living among
brute beasts" (St. Ignatius).

Wallace Stevens could see beauty in a city dump. But the place
he saw was transfigured by moonlight, and he condemned no
one to live with what he wrote of. But what happens to people
who are condemned to live and die in the places we have seen?
And, more to the point, what happens to the chiefs of society,
who allow such conditions to prevail; indeed, whose power of
place depends exactly on the existence of such places? To all

appearances, the twenty First Families of Peru seem far indeed from the fate of Job. They are neither stricken by God, nor driven by frenzy to curse Him. They exemplify what is in many cases a kind of blasphemy and a kind of judgment of God, for they are "good Catholics." Of the import of that, we shall see hereafter.

We have heard of a bishop in a poor diocese who asks $175 for a wedding in the cathedral. He wears a train some sixty feet long, never appears in the slum areas, and is known to live with a certain insistence upon personal comfort. We concelebrated this morning in a parish church where the pastor read the bishop's Lenten letter to his people. His words spoke much of heaven and more of hell, and urged, among other virtues, that Christians "be resigned to the social condition in which they were born." This in a diocese where Indians from the mountain areas live on ten or five cents a day and chew coco leaves to immunize themselves from cold and hunger. The people were also urged strongly to fast and pray. For many of them, nature and feudalism had already conspired to ensure the first benefit. And no bishop could teach them the second, so long as the Church herself invested in their misery.

We spent most of the day in the Monton slum. I suddenly came from great perplexity into a kind of peace. Sick at the stomach, eyes smarting from the smoke of spontaneous combustion arising here and there and settling in a pall upon the whole area. Was the peace a spurious one? In any case, it was as though God were trying to say:

> Try to understand that these conditions are a Biblical condition. They are joined to the life of Job, of Jeremiah, to the death of Isaiah and the death of Jesus. Try to understand further that my hidden mercy is never less hidden than here. Try also to understand that I have led my people as pioneers to this place, as a desert encampment, to form in them the fiber of heroes—steadfastness, freedom from illusion, isolation from the corrupt possession of the earth, love, and detachment. Understand also that you are led here for this purpose: to know in such a place as perhaps nowhere else that a future is being formed for you and others. In these people, in the few who share their fate, a new exodus is under way, a new form of death which always precedes birth.

In the eyes of a young priest, weak from illness, reflecting for all who could see the rewards of the Beatitudes, I seem to see what was meant by the Apocalypse: to stand where one must stand, to plant the landmarks by which the unborn will be enabled to walk (Rev. 2; 1, 9, 19).